Jeanne Jones

ENTERTAINS

Jeanne Jones
ENTERTAINS

Cook It Light Menus
for Every Occasion

Photographs by Jim Coit

CROWN PUBLISHERS, INC. NEW YORK

ALSO BY JEANNE JONES

The Calculating Cook

More Calculated Cooking

Diet for a Happy Heart

Secrets of Salt Free Cooking

Stuffed Spuds:
100 Meals in a Baked Potato

The Fabulous High Fiber Diet

Food Lovers' Diet

Cook It Light

Designed by Nancy Kenmore

Text copyright © 1991 by Jeanne Jones, Inc.

Photographs copyright © 1991 by Jim Coit

Published by Crown Publishers, Inc., 201 East 50th Street, New York, New York, 10022. Member of the Crown Publishing Group.

CROWN is a trademark of Crown Publishers, Inc.

Manufactured in Japan

Library of Congress Cataloging-in-Publication Data

Jones, Jeanne.
Jeanne Jones entertains/by Jeanne Jones: photographs by
Jim Coit
p.   cm.
Includes indexes.
1. Cookery.   2. Entertaining.   I. Title.
TX714.J652   1991   90-28381
641.5—dc20   CIP
ISBN 0-517-57522-1

1 3 5 7 9 10 8 6 4 2

First Edition

ACKNOWLEDGMENTS

For their help on this book, I'd like to thank Kate Adams, Caroline Avolino, Bradley Chamberlin, Donald Breitenberg, Tracy De Mas, Richard Duffy, William Hansen, Erica Marcus, Ken Sansone, Amy Boorstein, Nancy Kenmore, Joan Denman, Margaret McBride, Ed Washington, and Theodor Geisel.

I'd like to extend a special thanks to the following for table settings: The Dining Room Shop, La Jolla; I. Magnin, La Jolla Village Square; Linens, Linens, La Jolla; Robert Faine Faust, Private Collection.

TO WILLIAM HANSEN,
*for continuing to share
his many talents*

Contents

Introduction

I love food. I love everything about it. I love to eat. I love to cook and I love to entertain. In fact, entertaining is my favorite hobby as well as the basis for my career.

I also love to look good, feel good, and have lots of energy. I really do want to have it all. I want to be able to enjoy glorious food and glowing health at the same time—and I want to share my philosophy on how to do it.

Most people I meet are well aware of the importance of good nutrition and almost all of them are taking positive steps to do something about it—until they entertain! Then the high-fat hors d'oeuvres are passed, the salad gets a thick, creamy dressing, the usually broiled entree is cooked in sauce, and the steamed vegetables are topped with butter. Even the fresh fruit for dessert gets baked into a pie and served with ice cream. These people are "killing" their company in their attempt to please and impress. The more important the company, the harder they try.

Remember the Golden Rule! Think of "company" as a two-sided coin. The flip side is "guest." That is when you become someone else's company. How do you like to be entertained? Do you like to feel that you have to give up eating a day ahead of time to get ready for a party, or that you should fast for at least a day afterwards to get over it? Of course not!

The next time you are planning a party menu, pretend you are going to be the guest. In other words, design your menu as if you were going to be someone else's "company." You will be amazed at the difference it will make in your menu and how appreciative your guests will be.

To help you get started, I have written this book as a truly practical guide for personal entertaining. It is designed to help you plan parties of all types and sizes in your own home *and* doing your own cooking.

Your personal touch is what makes your parties special. Use your imagination, and use every room in your house as a possible entertainment center. It doesn't matter how small or how large your own home is—learning how to use the space you have in innovative ways is what is important for successful entertaining. You don't have to rent a room or borrow china, crystal, and silver, or even hire a caterer in order to have a successful party.

We all consider an invitation for a meal at someone's home the ultimate compliment. Why not pay this special compliment to your family and friends as often as you can? You will have a wonderful time, make a lot of other people happy, and enjoy becoming the most popular host or hostess you know.

PLANNING YOUR PARTY

Giving a party of any size can be lots of fun—rather than just lots of work—if you plan ahead properly. When planning a party, the first and most important thing to consider is the guest list. The type of party you give may differ greatly depending on the guests you invite. For example, you may have an elderly friend who is a delightful conversationalist and would enjoy a small sit-down dinner but not a stand-up cocktail party.

When selecting guests for a small dinner party, I find it is sometimes more fun to combine people who do not see one another regularly and who are involved in totally different fields.

It is also important and considerate to invite your guests far enough in advance so that they can work your party into their schedules. When possible invite your guests two to three weeks ahead of time. It is always disappointing to plan a party and find that everyone you especially wanted to come is already busy.

An invitation can be as simple as picking up the telephone and inviting a friend over for a meal, or as formal as an engraved invitation with an enclosed response card. There are also lots of clever invitations available for all occasions. Whether you are buying your invitations, making them yourself, or having them done for you, the important thing is that the invitation match the mood and theme of your party.

Unless I am planning a fairly large party I often invite my guests by telephone and then send a reminder a few days before the party confirming the date, time, place, and type of party. This way I get an immediate yes or no, and it is easier to assemble a compatible group. Also, it gives me the perfect opportunity to find out about any special dietary needs of my guests, ranging from simple likes and dislikes to food allergies.

This is an example of the kind of reminder I usually send:

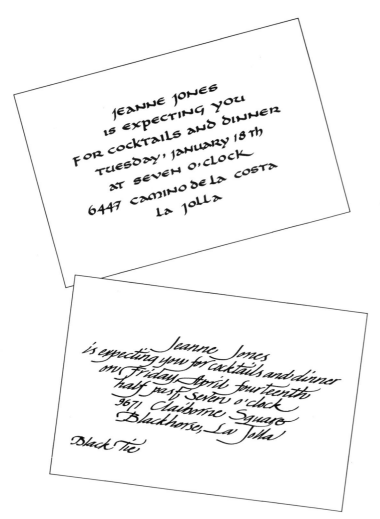

I never specify cocktails at one time and dinner at another, such as cocktails at 7:30 and dinner at 8:30. I like to think of the entire evening as just one party with one activity flowing naturally into another. I always allow time for my guests who may not know each other to get acquainted before sitting down for dinner together. This time is equally valuable for guests who are old friends to have an opportunity to catch up with each other's activities, particularly if they are not seated together at the table.

When receiving an invitation yourself, it is important always to respond as quickly as possible, giving the host or hostess an opportunity to ask someone else in your place.

After determining the type of party you are going to have and inviting your guests, the next consideration is the menu. Like the guest list, the menu is in part dictated by the type of party you are giving and also by the amount of help you are going to have.

If you are giving a dinner party by yourself, without any additional help, plan a menu that you can prepare ahead of time so you are free to enjoy your guests. As a host or hostess you are not simply preparing a meal; you are entertaining the people you invited. Planning a menu that you can serve easily makes your guests feel much more at ease than if you are continually jumping up and down from the table.

I prefer a sit-down dinner party for eight to ten people over all other types of entertaining. It is large enough to create a real party atmosphere and yet small enough for you to do all of the cooking yourself, without feeling as if you have gone into the catering business. It is also a small enough group for the entire table to be engaged in the same conversation.

When I am giving a small dinner party without any help I arrange the courses so that I am away from the table as little as possible. Sometimes I serve a first course of soup in a mug in the living room. This allows me to mingle graciously with my guests while removing their cocktail glasses and the hors d'oeuvres. Then I don't have to clear the area after dinner if I have planned to have my guests return to the living room for coffee or after-dinner drinks.

Another approach is to seat your guests for their first course, which may be an appetizer, soup, or salad, and ask them to help themselves to their entree, set out on a buffet next to the table or, for a more informal approach, left in pots on the stove. This gives you an opportunity to clear the table of the first course and tidy up the kitchen while your guests serve themselves. Then as you later remove their dinner plates, it is very easy to rinse each plate and put it in the dishwasher as it is cleared from the table; you have thus eliminated a horrendous mess in the kitchen when the party is over.

For a party of this type, I always finish with a dessert such as poached fruit, fresh fruit and cheese, or a cold soufflé, served at the table. The mood is much more formal than at an entire meal served buffet style, and by serving dinner in this manner, you are not away from the table as often. Also, when I am entertaining without help, I always ask one of my guests to serve the wine for me.

When giving a more formal dinner party with additional help, let your imagination run wild while planning the menu. Always include at least one dish you have never served before. Offering something new at a dinner party is far more exciting than sticking with the old favorites, just as it is more fun to wear something new.

I always love to have one course that is unusual, served in dishes not often used, such as "bowls" of hollowed-out artichokes filled with a chilled jelled soup and served on artichoke plates. After serving artichokes or any other "messy" course, finger bowls are important and certainly add a lovely touch to a formal dinner party. However, whenever you use finger bowls, change your guests' napkins afterwards. What could be more uncomfortable than a soggy napkin in your lap for the duration of the meal?

It is impossible to plan a menu, to shop, to cook, and to give the party all on the same day. (That is, it is impossible if you want to enjoy the party yourself.) Remember, entertaining should be exciting rather than exhausting.

A rule of thumb in party planning, whether it is for a formal dinner party or a backyard barbecue, is to plan your menu two to four days prior to the party and if possible do most of your shopping at least two days before. Last-minute shopping should only be for items such as fresh seafood or other perishable ingredients. The day before the party, prepare as many dishes as possible, leaving only those requiring last-minute preparation to just before the party begins.

When planning menus, balance the flavors, textures, and colors of the dishes you are going to serve. The same ingredients and seasonings should not be used in every course. Instead, the flavors of each dish should complement each other.

Variety in texture is also important. If you are going to serve a creamy quiche or soufflé as an entree, a crunchy salad is a better appetizer than a creamed soup. Different textures within the same dish also make it more interesting: raw vegetables, sprouts, nuts, and seeds are marvelous in leafy salads. Toasted croutons or bread crumbs can add both taste and texture to any dish.

Mixing colors certainly makes for more attractive presentation. Broiled chicken, mashed potatoes, and cauliflower can all be delicious, but because they are similar in color, they don't make a pretty picture when served on a plate together.

I like to use a theme when planning menus. International menus such as Italian, Spanish, French, Middle Eastern, or Oriental are fun and easily integrated into your table decor. You can do the same with American regional menus, as I have done in this book with its Southwestern-, Midwestern-, and Southern-inspired menus.

You can use a color theme for both the food and the decor, as I did for the Black and White After-the-Theater Champagne Supper (page 113) and the Christmas Cocktail Party (page 145). Or let whimsy run wild and plan truly outrageous and fun menus like the Ultimate Chocolate Fantasy Brunch (page 51) or the St. Patrick's Day Potatoes on Parade (page 159) menus. A well-conceived theme can make food fun and the focal point of the party.

After planning the menu inventory what you will need for the party and make your shopping list. Your list should be divided into categories to make shopping easier and more efficient. Include nonfood items as well, such as candles, flowers, and paper products. If any of these items needs to be bought on the day of the party, try ordering them ahead of time so they will be ready when you need them.

Decide how you will serve the menu you've designed. Check the table linens you plan to use, making sure they are clean and pressed. If you are giving a more casual party with paper cloths and napkins, put those items on the shopping list.

Next, consider your china, flatware, and serving pieces. If you don't have enough china in the same pattern for all of your guests, mix the patterns. It is less expensive than renting, less trouble than borrowing, and often creates a more interesting table.

The amount of stemware you need depends entirely on what you are serving to drink. If serving more than one wine, there should be a different wine glass for each. Always include water goblets as well as wine glasses; a guest not wishing to drink wine or wanting water as well should not have to ask for it.

Having the appropriate serving pieces for everything you plan to serve is not necessary. It is sometimes fun to use innovative containers such as large bowls filled with crushed ice for wine coolers and chilled soup tureens for salad. I have even filled large wine goblets with salad for luncheons. Always chill the salad plates or bowls so that they are cold when the salad is served.

Set your table as far in advance of your party as possible. It is an easy way to eliminate one of the last-minute frustrations of too much to do and too little time to do it. Once I have the table set, I can relax and concentrate on getting the meal and myself ready for the guests.

The rules for setting a table are easy and sensible. The flatware should be arranged in order of use from the outside in, with the forks on the left. On the right, the knives go next to the plate with the spoons to their right. The dessert spoon and fork may be placed above the plate.

I always arrange the dessert spoon and fork according to what I am serving for dessert. For example, if the primary implement is the spoon, then I put the spoon directly above the plate, with the dessert fork behind it; if the fork is going to be used first, then I reverse their positions. If I am serving a dish of ice milk and guests only need a spoon, then I omit the fork altogether.

When I use service plates for formal dinner parties, I usually place the napkins on the plates. If the first course is already on the plate when the guests are to be seated, then the napkins are placed to the left of the forks.

There are no strict rules as to how the napkins should be folded. I always iron them flat so that I can either fold them, use napkins rings or clips, or tie them with ribbons.

There was a time when wine glasses were arranged to the right of the water goblet in order of use from the inside out. I find that it is easier to pour the wine when the glasses are ordered from the outside in.

After the basic table is set, add your personal touches such as flowers, place cards, candles, menus, or table favors. Flowers should either be low enough to see over them or raised up on pedestals so that your guests can see under them. Never use flower arrangements that block the view across the table. If you are giving party favors, they can be as elegant or whimsical as you wish. For ladies' luncheons I often tie the place cards to bud vases filled with flowers, and give them to my guests as they leave. Hand-lettered menus add a personal touch to the table decor and also make nice favors.

Guests	Accept ✓ Refuse X	Seating Chart

Occasion _____

Place _____

Day _____

Date _____ Time _____

Checklist:

☐ Invitations _____
☐ Reminders _____
☐ Menu _____
☐ Table Linens _____
☐ China _____

☐ Crystal _____
☐ Silver _____

☐ Serving Pieces _____

☐ Flowers _____
☐ Table Decorations _____

☐ Candles _____
☐ Place Cards _____
☐ Favors _____

☐ Shopping List _____

Rentals _____

Help _____

Costs:	Budgeted	Actual
Food		
Wine		
Liquor		
Flowers		
Rentals		
Help		
Other		

Menu

Wines:

Liquor and Liqueurs: _____

Dress:
Hostess _____
Host _____

Review:

Keeping records of your parties provides you with a marvelous diary of all of your past entertaining, and is also a valuable resource in planning future parties. This is a sample page of my record-keeping book. It includes space for listing all the information you might wish to remember. I include a seating chart so that I avoid seating a guest by the same person each time he or she is invited.

A breakdown of both budgeted and actual costs is helpful in estimating expenses for future parties. It is also helpful in keeping accurate records for business entertaining, including the guests and a breakdown of the costs.

The records you keep can be as simple or as elaborate as you wish. By keeping records you will not only avoid repetitions such as serving the same food or wearing the same clothes but you will add variety to your parties in many ways—like using different linens, china, or centerpieces, or perhaps even serving in a different area of your house.

Now, on to preparing all the glorious food that is going to grace your beautiful table.

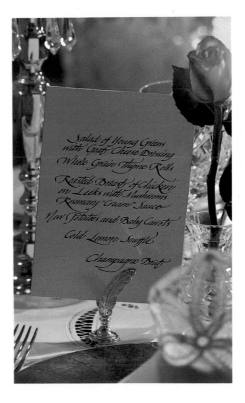

BREAKFAST

Breakfast reflects personal food preferences and life-long eating habits more than any other meal. Yet many people skip breakfast altogether in an attempt to control their weight. This is an enormous mistake. First, it doesn't work. Second, research indicates that people have more energy and perform better when they eat breakfast. In fact, research has proved that schoolchildren who routinely eat a good breakfast earn higher marks than those who don't. My favorite quotation on the subject is, "People who try to lose weight by skipping breakfast end up *fat* and *mean*!"

Basic but Chic

Orange Juice

*Goblet of "Good" Dry Cereal
with Fresh Berries*

Low-fat Vanilla Milk

Nothing is easier, faster, or more healthful for breakfast than a whole-grain cereal with milk and fresh fruit; however, it rarely comes to mind as a breakfast for company.

A couple of years ago I glamorized this simple approach to the morning meal. I was scheduled to demonstrate low-fat cereal toppings on the noon news in West Palm Beach, Florida. About ten minutes before I was to go on, live, I realized I didn't have any bowls. I did have goblets for a later demonstration of blender drinks, so I just put the dry cereal in the goblets and suggested to the viewers that this was an excellent way to gussy up an old standby: "If you find you are having guests unexpectedly and don't have anything in the house, just put your cereal in an elegant goblet and serve the milk in a fancy pitcher on the side."

As often happens, innovation and imagination saved the day. The audience loved the idea. The station got lots of calls from happy viewers who were delighted with the "helpful hint."

GOBLET OF "GOOD" DRY CEREAL WITH FRESH BERRIES

⅔ cup small shredded-wheat biscuits
⅓ cup fresh blueberries
⅓ cup fresh raspberries
1 cup Low-fat Vanilla Milk (recipe follows)

Place shredded-wheat biscuits in a large goblet and top with berries. Serve vanilla milk on the side.

MAKES 1 SERVING (WITH MILK)
Each serving contains approximately:
Calories: 295   Cholesterol: 6 mg
Fat: 1 g   Sodium: 199 mg

LOW-FAT VANILLA MILK

¾ cup water
½ cup instant nonfat dry milk powder
2 teaspoons frozen unsweetened apple juice concentrate, undiluted
¼ teaspoon vanilla extract

Combine all ingredients and mix well.

MAKES ONE 1-CUP SERVING
Each serving contains approximately:
Calories: 148   Cholesterol: 6 mg
Fat: Negligible   Sodium: 193 mg

All-American Classic

Melon Medley
Creamy Old-Fashioned Oatmeal
with Broiled Banana
and Vermont Maple Topping

My grandmother was a great advocate of oatmeal for a healthy breakfast, and current research indicates that she was right. For a real power start for school, work, or play, serve hot, Creamy Old-Fashioned Oatmeal topped with a broiled banana and a delicious maple-flavored topping. The broiled banana also makes an unusual and versatile side dish for fish, poultry, and meat. I even serve it for dessert, either by itself or on yogurt or ice milk. The Vermont Maple Topping is also good on yogurt and ice milk.

MELON MEDLEY

½ cup watermelon balls
½ cup cantaloupe balls

To serve, combine watermelon and cantaloupe balls.

MAKES 1 SERVING
Each serving contains approximately:
Calories: 54   Cholesterol: 0 mg
Fat: Negligible   Sodium: 9 mg

CREAMY OLD-FASHIONED OATMEAL WITH BROILED BANANA

2 cups cold water
⅔ cup old-fashioned rolled oats
⅛ teaspoon salt
1 banana, halved lengthwise
½ cup Vermont Maple Topping (recipe follows)

1. Combine cold water, rolled oats, and salt in a heavy saucepan and bring to a boil. Reduce heat and simmer for 5 minutes. Remove from heat and cover until it has thickened to the desired consistency, about 5 minutes.

2. Place banana, cut side up, on a baking sheet and place under broiler. Broil until lightly browned and bubbling. Watch carefully as banana will burn easily.

3. Spoon ¾ cup hot oatmeal into each of 2 bowls. Top each serving with a broiled half-banana and half the maple topping.

MAKES TWO ¾-CUP SERVINGS
Each serving contains approximately:
Calories: 219   Cholesterol: 13 mg
Fat: 5 g   Sodium: 204 mg

VERMONT MAPLE TOPPING

I always make more of this topping than I am planning to use because I like to have it on hand. It is a wonderful topping for toast, yogurt, ice milk, and the like.

1 cup low-fat ricotta cheese
3 tablespoons frozen unsweetened apple juice concentrate, undiluted
¾ teaspoon vanilla extract
⅜ teaspoon maple extract

Combine all ingredients in a blender container and blend until *satin* smooth. Store tightly covered in refrigerator.

MAKES 1½ CUPS; SIX ¼-CUP SERVINGS
Each serving contains approximately:
Calories: 75   Cholesterol: 13 mg
Fat: 3 g   Sodium: 54 mg

Beautiful Beginning

❖

Broiled Grapefruit

Texas Toast with Peach Butter

Turkey Sausage Patties

There is no more elegant way to start the day than with breakfast in bed. Surprise your loved one or your houseguests with this hearty, healthy, and delicious morning menu.

BROILED GRAPEFRUIT

I learned this preparation and presentation for broiled grapefruit from a sushi chef in Japan. It is not only much more attractive than plain-old halved grapefruit but it is also much easier to eat. Broiling the grapefruit brings out all its natural sweetness, so you don't need sugar.

1 grapefruit
2 fresh raspberries, for garnish (optional)

1. Cut off a wide piece of the top and bottom ends of the grapefruit, exposing the inner pith; reserve the ends. Cut grapefruit in half horizontally, then hollow out each half, forming two rings of peel. Place a reserved end inside each ring, cut side up, and press down, creating a bottom for each "bowl."

2. Dice the peeled fruit and spoon it into the grapefruit bowls. Set the bowls on a baking sheet and place under a broiler until lightly browned.

3. Top each broiled grapefruit with a raspberry and serve.

MAKES 2 SERVINGS
Each serving contains approximately:
Calories: 44   Cholesterol: 0 mg
Fat: Negligible   Sodium: 0 mg

How to Prepare
Broiled Grapefruit

❖

1. Slice off both ends of the grapefruit.

2. Cut the grapefruit in half, down the middle.

5. Now you have a grapefruit peel ring.

6. Fit the grapefruit end and ring together, forming a bowl.

3. Here are the grapefruit halves and ends.

4. Cut the fruit away from the peel.

7. Dice the fruit removed in Step 5.

8. And place the diced fruit into the bowls, which are then broiled.

TEXAS TOAST

In Texas many restaurants roll their French toast in corn flakes and call it "Texas Toast." My variation on the theme is to use naturally sweetened amaranth flakes, which are usually available in health food stores and are more flavorful and more nutritious than corn flakes. However, you can get the same wonderfully crunchy texture from any naturally sweetened whole-grain cereal.

> 2 egg whites, beaten until frothy
> 1 tablespoon nonfat (skim) milk
> 1½ teaspoons frozen unsweetened apple
>   juice concentrate, undiluted
> 2 slices whole-grain bread
> ½ cup amaranth flakes

1. Combine the egg whites, milk, and apple juice concentrate in a bowl and mix well.

2. Place the bread in a bowl just large enough to hold it. Pour the egg mixture over the bread and allow it to soak in. Turn bread over and allow to stand until all liquid is absorbed.

3. Top each slice of soaked bread with 2 tablespoons amaranth flakes and press them in. Place bread flaked side down in a large, hot skillet sprayed with nonstick vegetable coating or in a nonstick skillet. Top each slice of bread with 2 tablespoons amaranth flakes, pressing them in. Cook bread until well browned, about 5 minutes. Turn over carefully with a spatula and brown the other side, about 5 minutes.

4. To serve, cut each slice of Texas Toast in quarters on the diagonal and place 4 triangles of toast on each of 2 plates. Place a cooked Turkey Sausage Patty (page 26) in the center of each plate. Top each toast quarter with 1 tablespoon of Peach Butter (page 26). Garnish each plate with 4 peach slices and a mint sprig.

MAKES 2 SERVINGS
Each serving contains approximately:
Calories: 154   Cholesterol: 1 mg
Fat: 1 g   Sodium: 180 mg

PEACH BUTTER

This fruit butter is not only good on Texas Toast but it is a great substitute for both butter and jam on toast, pancakes, and waffles, and is sensational on a peanut butter sandwich.

> 8 ounces dried, unsulfured peaches (2
>   cups)
> 1 12-ounce can frozen unsweetened
>   apple juice concentrate, undiluted
>   (1½ cups)
> 1½ cups water
> 1 teaspoon ground cinnamon

Combine all ingredients in a heavy saucepan and bring to a boil. Reduce heat and simmer, uncovered, for 30 minutes. Allow to cool slightly and then spoon into a food processor with a metal blade, and blend until satin smooth. Store, covered, in the refrigerator.

MAKES 2 CUPS; 8 ¼-CUP SERVINGS
Each serving contains approximately:
Calories: 187   Cholesterol: 0 mg
Fat: 1 g   Sodium: 16 mg

TURKEY SAUSAGE PATTIES

These spicy patties add the perfect taste balance for this breakfast menu. They also make great turkey burgers and are good crumbled over rice or pasta. I always make the whole recipe, then freeze what is left in small balls to use in my Gift-Wrapped Sausages (page 148).

> 1 pound lean ground turkey
> 1½ teaspoons dried sage, crushed
> ½ teaspoon garlic powder
> ½ teaspoon onion powder
> ½ teaspoon mace
> ½ teaspoon freshly ground black pepper
> ⅛ teaspoon ground allspice
> ⅛ teaspoon ground cloves

1. Combine all ingredients in a food processor with a metal blade and blend until well mixed.

2. Divide sausage mixture into 8 patties. (To keep patties for future use, wrap tightly and freeze, or roll into small balls and freeze.)

3. Place patties in a hot skillet that has been coated with nonstick vegetable spray or use a nonstick skillet and brown patties on both sides about 3 to 4 minutes per side.

MAKES 8 SINGLE-PATTY SERVINGS
Each serving contains approximately:
Calories: 70   Cholesterol: 37 mg
Fat: 2 g   Sodium: 40 mg

Here I've used a pastry bag to pipe the Peach Butter onto the Texas
Toast for a prettier presentation.

Morning Meeting

❖

Fresh Brewed Coffee

Selection of Teas

Fresh Juice

Blueberry–Oat Bran Muffins

*Molasses–Wheat Bran Muffins with Raisins
and Vanilla Cream Spread (page 53)*

*Cinnamon Waffle "Designer" Sandwiches
with Peanut Butter Cream Spread
and Peach Butter (page 26)*

You have volunteered to have the morning meeting at your house. Whether it's a get-acquainted coffee for a political candidate, the fund-raising committee meeting for your favorite charity, or a board meeting of your school or church, the first question is always the same: "What should I serve with the coffee?"

If you're hosting an early meeting you can safely assume that many members of the group will not have had breakfast. For this reason, I like to serve a selection of hearty breakfast breads with tasty and unusual spreads. I always offer fresh fruit juice, both regular and decaffeinated coffee, and a selection of teas.

Here's a meeting menu that can be prepared the night before, allowing you the time to get both your house and yourself ready for your early-morning guests.

Some people prefer to serve tea with honey rather than sugar.

BLUEBERRY–OAT BRAN MUFFINS

The secret to success with the Blueberry–Oat Bran Muffins is to use frozen blueberries: they will thaw as they bake and plump up in the muffins. If thawed before baking, they shrivel up as they bake. (By the way, both muffins here freeze beautifully. Let them cool to room temperature, then freeze immediately in either Zip-lock bags or wrapped airtight in plastic wrap or aluminum foil. Reheat the aluminum foil-wrapped muffins for about 15 minutes in a 350°F. oven or the plastic-wrapped muffins in the microwave oven—the time for the latter depends on the number of muffins and the wattage of your oven.) These and the wheat bran muffins can be made with nonfat (skim) milk instead of buttermilk by also substituting 1 tablespoon of baking powder for the 1 teaspoon of baking soda. I use buttermilk and baking soda because I think the muffins have a slightly better texture.

2⅔ cups oat bran
½ teaspoon salt
1 teaspoon baking soda
1 teaspoon ground cinnamon
2 egg whites, lightly beaten

1 teaspoon vanilla extract
2 tablespoons canola or corn oil
½ cup frozen unsweetened apple juice
    concentrate, undiluted
⅔ cup buttermilk
1 cup frozen blueberries

1. Preheat the oven to 400°F. Spray a standard (¼-cup) muffin tin with nonstick vegetable coating.

2. In a bowl, combine the oat bran, salt, baking soda, and cinnamon; mix well.

3. In another bowl, combine the egg whites, vanilla, oil, apple juice concentrate, and buttermilk. Pour the liquid mixture into the dry mixture, add the frozen blueberries, and mix just enough to moisten dry ingredients. *Do not overmix!*

4. Spoon batter into prepared muffin tin. Bake for 18 minutes or until lightly browned. Do not overcook; muffins should be moist when they come out of the oven.

MAKES 12 STANDARD MUFFINS
Each muffin contains approximately:
Calories: 119   Cholesterol: Negligible
Fat: 4 g   Sodium: 198 mg

I garnish trays of juice with either fresh mint leaves or flowers.

MOLASSES-WHEAT BRAN MUFFINS WITH RAISINS

1½ cups unprocessed wheat bran
1 cup whole wheat flour
1 teaspoon baking soda
½ teaspoon salt
⅔ cup raisins
2 egg whites, lightly beaten
2 tablespoons canola or corn oil
¼ cup unsulfured molasses
1½ cups buttermilk

1. Preheat the oven to 400°F. Spray a standard (¼-cup) muffin tin with nonstick vegetable coating.

2. In a bowl, combine all dry ingredients and mix thoroughly. Be certain that all lumps are out of baking soda. Sprinkle the raisins over the mixture and set aside.

3. Mix the liquid ingredients thoroughly.

4. Pour the liquid mixture into the dry mixture and mix just enough to moisten. (It is very important to have both dry and liquid ingredients mixed very well when making muffins because when they are combined they should be mixed only enough to moisten the dry ingredients. Overmixing will ruin the light texture of the muffins.)

5. Spoon the batter into the prepared muffin tins and bake muffins for 18 minutes, or until lightly browned. Do not overcook; muffins should be moist when they come out of the oven. Serve with Vanilla Cream Spread (page 53).

MAKES 12 STANDARD MUFFINS
Each muffin (without spread) contains approximately:

Calories: 124   Cholesterol: 1 mg
Fat: 3 g   Sodium: 217 mg

If you pipe all of the spreads onto individual leaves, your guests can serve themselves without destroying the presentation. Here I've chilled the Peanut Butter Cream Spread, Vanilla Cream Spread, and the Peach Butter so that they hold their shape.

Cinnamon Waffle "Designer" Sandwiches

Since waffles are like bread slices, I use these Cinnamon Waffles to make "designer" sandwiches filled with Peanut Butter Cream Spread and Peach Butter. The Peanut Butter Cream Spread and Peach Butter are also wonderful on pancakes, toast, bagels, and English muffins.

2 cups unbleached all-purpose flour
⅓ cup instant nonfat dry milk powder
1 tablespoon baking powder
½ teaspoon baking soda
½ teaspoon salt
1 tablespoon ground cinnamon
2 egg whites
¼ cup canola or corn oil
2 cups buttermilk

1. Spray a square waffle iron with nonstick vegetable spray. Preheat the iron according to the manufacturer's recommendations. (If you are using a small waffle iron, amount of batter for each waffle will be less and you will wind up with more waffles. Also cooking time varies greatly depending on type of waffle iron you are using.)

2. Combine the flour, milk powder, baking powder, baking soda, salt, and cinnamon in a bowl.

3. Combine the egg whites and oil, then add to the dry mixture. Stir in the buttermilk and blend with a spoon or rotary beater until well mixed.

4. Pour 1 cup of the mixture into the center of the 9-inch-square hot iron and bake until the steaming stops and waffle is golden brown, about 4 minutes. Make 2 more waffles.

5. To serve, cut each square on the diagonal to make 24 triangles. Spread half the triangles with the Peanut Butter Cream Spread (recipe follows) and half with Peach Butter (page 26). Join halfs to make 12 triangle-shaped sandwiches.

**MAKES THREE 9-INCH SQUARE WAFFLES;
12 SANDWICH SERVINGS**
Each serving contains approximately:
Calories: 141   Cholesterol: 2 mg
Fat: 5 g   Sodium: 363 mg

Peanut Butter Cream Spread

1¼ cups low-fat ricotta cheese
¼ cup unhomogenized peanut butter
2 teaspoons vanilla extract
½ teaspoon ground cinnamon
1 tablespoon sugar

Combine the ingredients in a food processor with a metal blade and blend until satin smooth.

**MAKES 1½ CUPS;
TWENTY-FOUR 1-TABLESPOON SERVINGS**
Each serving contains approximately:
Calories: 37   Cholesterol: 4 mg
Fat: 2 g   Sodium: 17 mg

BRUNCH

Although brunch, a contraction of the words *break-fast* and *lunch,* originally connoted a meal that was served later than breakfast but earlier than lunch, the Sunday brunch buffet served by many hotels, restaurants, and private clubs has gone a long way to redefine the word. These opulent spreads, usually served from ten in the morning until two in the afternoon, include every imaginable item found on a breakfast menu along with many dishes usually associated with lunch or dinner.

I don't like these midday eating extravaganzas. I always end up with too much of something I don't like, not enough of what I like best, and a bizarre combination of foods on my plate. I leave feeling uncomfortably full rather than happy and satisfied.

My brunch strategy is to decide whether the brunch meal is breakfast or lunch before I start. This way I don't end up with blueberry blintzes and beef stroganoff on the same plate. When planning a brunch menu for entertaining at home, I follow the same rule.

Make-Ahead Marvel

❖

Tomato-Citrus Cooler

*Zinfandel Poached Pears with
Spiced Cheese Sauce*

Chicken Ragout en Croustade

*Easy Whole Wheat–
Thyme Bread*

Weekends offer a wonderful opportunity to invite friends for brunch, and this Make Ahead Marvel is a perfect menu to serve when you are returning home along with your guests. Everything can be prepared ahead of time so that you can serve soon after you arrive, without much time away from your company.

TOMATO-CITRUS COOLER

❖

This Tomato-Citrus Cooler is both unusual and refreshing as it is, but also makes a delightfully different brunch cocktail. Use it as you would a Bloody Mary mix.

> 2 cups tomato juice
> 2 cups fresh orange juice
> 2 tablespoons fresh lime juice
> 8 drops Tabasco, or to taste
> 4 lime slices, for garnish (optional)

Combine all ingredients except lime slices and mix well. Chill well before serving.

MAKES 1 QUART; FOUR 1-CUP SERVINGS

Each serving contains approximately:
Calories: 79   Cholesterol: 0 mg
Fat: Negligible   Sodium: 360 mg

ZINFANDEL POACHED PEARS WITH SPICED CHEESE SAUCE

◆

The pears can be used for a dessert as well as an appetizer. When serving them for dessert, omit the peppercorns and serve them on Vanilla Cream Spread (page 53) instead of the cheese sauce.

> 4 ripe Bartlett pears
> 4 cinnamon sticks
> 12 black peppercorns
> 1 magnum (1.5 liters) white Zinfandel (about 8 cups)
> 1 cup Spiced Cheese Sauce (recipe follows)
> Ground cinnamon, for garnish (optional)

1. Using an apple corer, remove the core from the blossom end of each pear, being careful not to disturb the stem. Using a potato peeler, peel each pear as smooth as possible. Place the peeled, cored pears in a deep saucepan just large enough to hold the fruit. Add the cinnamon sticks and peppercorns, then pour in enough wine to cover the pears.

2. Bring the wine to a boil, reduce the heat, and simmer for 5 to 10 minutes, or until pears can be easily pierced with a fork. Cooking time depends on ripeness of pears. Remove from heat.

3. Allow the pears to cool in the wine to room temperature. Reserve 2 tablespoons of the pear poaching liquid to make the sauce, cover the pears, and refrigerate for 24 hours to give them time to absorb the color and flavor of the wine.

4. Spoon ¼ cup of the Spiced Cheese Sauce into the bottom of 4 shallow bowls. Place 1 pear, stem up, on each bed of sauce. (Reserve the poaching liquid to serve as a delicious, refreshing nonalcoholic beverage.) Sprinkle each serving with a touch of cinnamon, then serve.

MAKES 4 SERVINGS
Each serving contains approximately:
Calories: 200   Cholesterol: 19 mg
Fat: 6 g   Sodium: 79 mg

SPICED CHEESE SAUCE

> 1 cup low-fat ricotta cheese
> 2 tablespoons poaching liquid from pears
> ¼ teaspoon freshly grated nutmeg
> ¼ teaspoon mace

Combine the sauce ingredients in a food processor with a metal blade. Blend until *satin* smooth. If the sauce is too thick, add a little more of the poaching liquid.

MAKES 1 CUP; FOUR ¼-CUP SERVINGS
Each serving contains approximately:
Calories: 89   Cholesterol: 19 mg
Fat: 5 g   Sodium: 78 mg

CHICKEN STOCK

Your own homemade stock is not only tastier than store-bought, it's also far more economical since a fine stock can be made from scraps. And remember, making your own stock only takes 15 minutes of preparation. You will notice in the recipe that the carrots are peeled and the leaves are removed from the celery but that the onions and garlic are not peeled. The reason for this is that the outside of the carrot has been oxidized and therefore tends to add a bitter taste to the stock, as do the leaves of the celery. The onions are not peeled because the skins do not affect the taste of the stock; in fact, they add a little desirable color. Buy chicken for stock—wings, backs, and necks are good —from a butcher, or save your own leftover chicken carcasses and scraps in the freezer until you're ready to make stock.

> 3 to 5 pounds chicken bones, parts, and
>   giblets, excluding the liver
> 2 carrots, peeled and cut into pieces
> 2 celery ribs, without leaves, cut into
>   pieces
> 1 onion, unpeeled and quartered
> 2 to 4 garlic cloves, unpeeled and halved
> 3 parsley sprigs
> 1 bay leaf
> 12 peppercorns
> ¼ cup vinegar
>   Cold water to cover ingredients by at
>   least 3 inches

1. Put all the ingredients into a large pot with a lid. Add cold water to cover by at least 3 inches and bring slowly to a simmer.

2. Reduce the heat and cover the pot, leaving the cover askew. Simmer for at least 3 hours. (The longer you cook the stock, the more flavor it will have.)

3. Remove the pot from the heat. Remove and discard the chicken pieces and vegetables. (By this point, they'll have lost any flavor or nutritional value.) When it's cool enough to handle, strain the stock and cool to room temperature.

4. To defat the stock, refrigerate it until all the fat congeals on top. Then with a rubber spatula or wooden spoon, remove the fat.

5. Finally, pour the defatted stock into ice cube trays. When the cubes are frozen, store them in sealed plastic bags in your freezer. Each cube contains 2 tablespoons of stock.

**MAKES APPROXIMATELY
10 CUPS OF STOCK**

Each cup contains approximately:

Calories: Negligible   *Cholesterol: Negligible*
Fat: Negligible   *Sodium: Negligible*

NOTE: Nutritional composition of the stock will vary according to the exact amount of ingredients and the length of cooking time.

HOW TO MAKE CHICKEN STOCK

1. Assemble your ingredients.

2. Add cold water to cover.

3. Bring your stock slowly to a simmer. Cover the pot with the lid askew and cook at a slow simmer for at least 3 hours—the longer the better.

4. Strain the stock through a colander then discard the chicken bones and vegetables. Refrigerate stock uncovered until fat congeals on the top.

5. Using a rubber spatula or a spoon, carefully remove all the congealed fat.

6. Discard the fat.

7. Pour the defatted stock into ice cube trays and freeze. Store frozen stock cubes in sealed plastic bags in your freezer. Each cube equals 2 tablespoons of stock.

CHICKEN RAGOUT EN CROUSTADE

The day before serving, make the bread, hollow it out for croustades, and make the filling. If you don't have the time to bake the bread the day before, order small whole wheat loaves from your local bakery for the croustade shells. The chicken filling is also wonderful served over rice or pasta, and makes a delicious filling for an omelet.

4 (4-inch) round loaves Whole Wheat–
    Thyme Bread (recipe follows) or other
    whole-grain bread

FILLING
1 cup defatted Chicken Stock (recipe
    follows)
1 cup nonfat (skim) milk
2 tablespoons corn oil margarine
1 large shallot, minced (2 tablespoons)
2 tablespoons whole wheat flour
¼ teaspoon salt
½ pound fresh mushrooms, thinly sliced
    (2 cups)

1 tablespoon Madeira
2 cups diced cooked chicken breast
    (12 ounces raw)
1 cup diced cooked carrots
1 cup cooked tiny peas (if using frozen,
    thaw before using)
4 cups sunflower sprouts, for garnish
    (optional)

1. Slice the top off of each loaf of bread and set aside. Carefully hollow out each loaf, leaving walls ½ inch thick. (Reserve the center for croutons and crumbs.) Place the tops back on the loaves and wrap them tightly; set aside until you are ready to toast them the next day.

2. Combine the chicken stock and milk in a saucepan and bring to a simmer. In another pan, melt 1 tablespoon of the margarine and add the shallot. Cook until soft, then add the flour. Cook, stirring constantly, for 3 minutes. *Do not brown!* Add the simmering liquid all at once, stirring with a wire whisk. Continue cooking for 30 minutes, stirring occasionally. If the sauce is not thick enough, continue cooking a little longer. Add salt and mix well. Cover and set aside.

3. Melt the remaining tablespoon of margarine in a skillet and add the mushrooms. Cook over medium heat, stirring constantly, until mushrooms start to soften. Cover and cook for 5 minutes. Uncover and continue cooking over high heat until almost all liquid has evaporated. Add the Madeira and again cook until almost all the liquid is evaporated.

4. To the sauce add the mushrooms, chicken, carrots, and peas. Mix thoroughly, remove from heat, and allow to cool slightly. Cover tightly and refrigerate until ready to use.

5. Preheat the oven to 350°F. Place the loaves and tops, cut sides up, on a baking sheet. Spray all cut surfaces with nonstick vegetable spray, then bake for 15 to 20 minutes or until well toasted. While the croustades are toasting, reheat the filling to serving temperature. Fill each croustade with 1 cup of the filling, place the tops back on the loaves, and place loaves on serving dishes. Surround the loaves with a ring of sunflower sprouts.

MAKES 4 SERVINGS

Each serving contains approximately:

Calories: 350   *Cholesterol: 49 mg*

Fat: 11 g   *Sodium: 452 mg*

NOTE: Nutritional information assumes only the "lid" of the croustade and the filling will be eaten.

EASY WHOLE WHEAT–THYME BREAD

⅔ cup water

3 tablespoons corn oil margarine

1½ tablespoons sugar

⅔ cup nonfat (skim) milk, cold

2 envelopes (2 tablespoons) active dry yeast (check date on package before using)

3 egg whites, lightly beaten

¾ teaspoon salt

1 tablespoon dried thyme leaves, crushed with a mortar and pestle

4 cups whole wheat flour

½ cup oat bran

1. Bring the water to a boil in a saucepan. Remove from the heat and add the margarine and sugar. Stir until margarine melts, then add the milk and mix well. Pour the mixture over the yeast and set aside until yeast starts to bubble, about 10 minutes.

2. Combine the egg whites, yeast mixture, salt, and thyme in a large bowl and mix well. Add the flour, 1 cup at a time, and mix until well blended and the dough forms a ball. Place the dough ball in a bowl that has been coated with nonstick vegetable spray. Cover the bowl with a damp towel and allow to rise in a warm place until doubled in bulk, about 1 hour.

3. Sprinkle the oat bran on a board so that the dough will not stick to it. Punch the dough down flat and cut into quarters. Roll each quarter into a ball. Roll each ball in the oat bran. Place the balls on an ungreased baking sheet.

4. Preheat the oven to 350°F. Bake loaves for 35 minutes, or until golden brown in color and the loaves sound hollow when tapped.

VARIATION: *Whole Wheat–Thyme Rolls*

These rolls can be made any time and stored in sealed bags in the freezer. They are fabulous dinner rolls, because they freeze well, they require no kneading, and they are delicious. To defrost, wrap them in aluminum foil and heat in a 350°F. oven for 15 minutes or seal them in a plastic Zip-lock bag and heat them in a microwave oven for 1 to 2 minutes.

Divide dough into 34 1½-inch balls, and place on ungreased baking sheets. Bake for 20 minutes, or until golden brown.

MAKES FOUR 4-INCH LOAVES OR THIRTY-FOUR 2-INCH ROLLS

Each loaf or roll contains approximately:

	Loaf	Roll
Calories:	*569*	*67*
Fat:	*12 g*	*1 g*
Cholesterol:	*1 mg*	*Negligible*
Sodium:	*626 mg*	*74 mg*

Sunday Brunch

❖

Melon Medley (page 21)

My Eggs Benedict

Piña Colada

Traditionally, brunch is more popular as a meal shared by family and friends on Sunday than on any other day of the week. Also traditionally, egg dishes are the most popular Sunday brunch entree. For this Sunday brunch I have designed a lighter version of eggs Benedict. By significantly lowering the saturated fat, cholesterol, and sodium without altering the tastes and textures of this classic, we can all enjoy it in better health.

You can serve melon balls in just about anything. These glass baskets were perfect for an Easter theme.

Flowers make a more colorful garnish for Eggs Benedict than the traditional sliced truffle.

MY EGGS BENEDICT

❖

For a lighter version of eggs Benedict, sauté turkey breast with a touch of Liquid Smoke to achieve a taste similar to Canadian bacon, with less sodium and none of the nitrites. I use only the poached egg whites, as well. When topped with my hollandaise sauce, the overall taste is much the same yet the calories and cholesterol are much lower than the original. (An egg yolk contains about 60 calories and 213 milligrams of cholesterol.)

1 *tablespoon corn oil margarine*

½ *teaspoon Liquid Smoke (available in specialty stores and some supermarkets)*

12 *thin slices (1 ounce each) cooked turkey breast*

3 *cups Light Hollandaise Sauce (recipe follows)*

6 *homemade English Muffins, split and toasted (recipe follows)*

12 *Poached Egg Whites (recipe follows) Edible flowers, for garnish (optional)*

1. In a skillet over medium heat, melt the margarine. Add the Liquid Smoke and mix thoroughly. Place the turkey slices in the skillet and heat, turning frequently, until lightly browned on both sides, about 3 minutes.

2. Spread 1 tablespoon of hollandaise on each muffin half. Place a turkey slice on top of each, then place a poached egg white, rounded side up, on top of each turkey slice. Spoon 3 tablespoons sauce on top of each poached egg white and garnish with a flower, if desired.

MAKES 6 SERVINGS

Each serving contains approximately:

Calories: 394   *Cholesterol: 110 mg*

Fat: 19 g   *Sodium: 500 mg*

POACHED EGG WHITES

12 egg whites

1. Coat the insides of 12 egg poaching cups or custard cups with nonstick vegetable spray. Place an egg white into each cup.

2. Poach the whites either by putting the egg cups into an egg poacher over simmering water, or by putting the custard cups in a standard oven or microwave. Cook only long enough for the whites to turn solid white; overcooking will toughen them.

MAKES 12 EGG WHITES

Each egg white contains approximately:

Calories: 16   *Cholesterol: 0 mg*

Fat: Negligible   *Sodium: 50 mg*

ENGLISH MUFFINS

I always make my own English muffins, because I prefer them to the commercial kind. (Once while I was making them, a neighbor dropped by. She was surprised to find out that you could *make* English Muffins; she thought they only came in packages from the store.) I prefer using a mixture of half whole wheat flour and half white flour; the whole wheat adds a wonderful taste and texture. However, for more classic muffins you may want to use all unbleached flour.

To add additional color to the meal, serve fresh fruits. A medley of different colored melon balls looks like little Easter eggs in bowls.

1 cup nonfat (skim) milk, boiling

3 tablespoons corn oil margarine

2 tablespoons honey

1 envelope (1 tablespoon) active dry yeast (check date on package before using)

¼ cup lukewarm water

2 egg whites

¾ teaspoon salt

2 cups unbleached all-purpose flour

2 cups whole wheat flour

½ cup cornmeal

1. Combine the hot milk, margarine, and honey in a large mixing bowl and stir until the margarine melts. Allow the milk mixture to cool to lukewarm.

2. Combine the yeast and lukewarm water and allow to stand, out of a draft, until doubled in bulk. This takes only a few minutes.

3. Add the yeast mixture to the milk mixture. Combine the egg whites and salt, beat lightly, and add to milk mixture, blending well.

4. Slowly stir in the flours, a little at a time. When all the flour has been added, knead the dough in the bowl until well mixed. Remove dough to a floured board and knead until shiny and elastic, about 3 or 4 minutes.

5. Wash the bowl in which you mixed the dough, dry thoroughly, and coat with nonstick vegetable spray. Return dough to bowl and cover with a damp towel. Place in a warm spot and allow to rise until doubled in bulk, about 1½ hours.

6. Put the dough ball on a floured board, punch down, and knead again for a minute or two.

7. Sprinkle each of 2 baking sheets with ¼ cup of the cornmeal. Roll the dough out into a large circle ¼ inch thick and cut into 3½-inch rounds using a biscuit cutter. (The lid from a wide-mouthed jar will also work.) After cutting out 12 muffins, place them on the cornmeal-sprinkled cookie sheets. Then form the remaining dough back into a ball and again roll it out ¼ inch thick, cutting as many more muffins as possible and repeating this process until you have 20 muffin rounds in all.

8. Turn each muffin over to coat the other side with cornmeal. Cover both pans lightly with towels and allow to rise in a warm place until approximately double in height, about 45 minutes.

9. Lightly grease a griddle or large frying pan. Cook muffins over medium heat for approximately 8 to 10 minutes on each side. Cool muffins on a rack.

MAKES 20 MUFFINS

Each muffin contains approximately:

Calories: 122   *Cholesterol: Negligible*

Fat: 2 g   *Sodium: 124 mg*

LIGHT HOLLANDAISE SAUCE

The Light Hollandaise Sauce receives most of its volume from the beaten egg whites, therefore it must be used as soon as possible after it is made or it will collapse. The sauce is also delicious on steamed vegetables, fish, and poultry.

    2   egg yolks
    2   tablespoons fresh lemon juice
    ⅛   teaspoon salt
        Pinch cayenne pepper
    6   tablespoons corn oil margarine, melted
    3   egg whites
    ⅛   teaspoon cream of tartar

1. Place the egg yolks, lemon juice, salt, and cayenne in a blender container. Cover the blender and blend at high speed for 2 to 3 seconds. Reduce speed to medium. Remove the lid but leave the blender running and slowly pour in melted margarine in a very thin stream. Set aside. (If you are not going to use the sauce immediately, set the blender container into a pan of lukewarm water so that the sauce will not separate.)

2. Combine the egg whites and cream of tartar and beat until soft peaks form. Gradually fold the sauce mixture into the egg whites until it is smooth but still a very light mixture. Use immediately!

MAKES 3 CUPS; SIX ½-CUP SERVINGS

Each serving contains approximately:

    Calories: 131   Cholesterol: 71 mg
    Fat: 13 g   Sodium: 216 mg

PIÑA COLADA

The tropical tastes of pineapple and coconut combine in this nonalcoholic Piña Colada to blend well with the other flavors in this menu. To avoid the highly saturated fat in real coconut, the Piña Colada is made with coconut extract and low-fat milk. It tastes amazingly like the real thing, delicious straight or used as a mix for a rum or vodka morning cocktail.

    2   cups low-fat milk
    2   cups unsweetened pineapple juice
    1   tablespoon vanilla extract
    1   tablespoon coconut extract
    2   tablespoons sugar
    4   fresh pineapple wedges, for garnish
        (optional)

Combine all ingredients except garnish in a blender container and blend on high speed until frothy. Pour into 6 tall glasses over ice cubes. Garnish with pineapple wedges on rim of glass, if desired.

MAKES SIX ⅔-CUP SERVINGS

Each serving contains approximately:

    Calories: 106   Cholesterol: 6 mg
    Fat: 2 g   Sodium: 42 mg

Ultimate Chocolate Fantasy

❖

Chocolate Waffles

Chocolate Crepes
with Cinnamon-Apple Filling
and Vanilla Cream Spread

Heart-Healthy Chocolate Muffins

Chocolate French Toast

Chocolate Bread Pudding
with Caramel Sauce

Creamy Vanilla Sauce

Chocolate Sauce

Fresh Berry Sauce

In spite of the fact that everything in this menu is chocolate, there is almost no cholesterol and it is very low in saturated fat, calories, and sodium. Imagine titillating your guests with this display of decadence that they can enjoy without the usual guilt —or just serve one or two of these tasty chocolate treats for your next gathering and add a marvelous touch of whimsy to your party. For instance, both the Chocolate Crepes with Cinnamon-Apple Filling and the Chocolate Bread Pudding with Caramel Sauce can lead double lives as delicious desserts. I also use the sauces with fresh or poached fruit as desserts for other menus in this book.

O P P O S I T E : The top of a piano works beautifully as a buffet table. **R I G H T :** If you have a waffle iron that makes interesting shapes, by all means use it.

CHOCOLATE WAFFLES

2 cups whole wheat flour
½ cup unsweetened cocoa powder, sifted
½ cup sugar
1 teaspoon ground cinnamon
2 teaspoons baking powder
½ teaspoon salt
1 cup nonfat (skim) milk
¼ cup canola or corn oil
1 tablespoon vanilla extract
3 egg whites, beaten until stiff but not dry

1. Combine flour, cocoa powder, sugar, cinnamon, baking powder, and salt and mix well. Set aside.

2. Combine the milk, oil, and vanilla; mix well and add to the dry mixture. Again mix well. Fold in the beaten egg whites, being careful not to overmix.

3. Preheat a waffle iron and coat with nonstick vegetable spray. Pour ½ cup waffle batter into the center of the hot iron and bake for about 6 minutes or until desired crispness.

4. Continue to make waffles, keeping others warm by placing them in a covered dish in a 250°F. oven.

MAKES 10 WAFFLES
Each waffle contains approximately:
Calories: 197   Cholesterol: Negligible
Fat: 7 g   Sodium: 281 mg

CHOCOLATE CREPES WITH CINNAMON-APPLE FILLING AND VANILLA CREAM SPREAD

This combination of flavors—chocolate, cinnamon-apple, and vanilla—is a real winner. But I've found dozens of uses for each of the components in this dish as well.

Chocolate Crepes (recipe follows)
Cinnamon-Apple Filling (recipe follows)
Vanilla Cream Spread (page 53)

To assemble, spoon ¼ cup filling down the center of each crepe. Fold crepe over filling and place seam side down on a serving dish. Top each crepe with 1 tablespoon of the Vanilla Cream Spread.

MAKES 12 SERVINGS
Each serving contains approximately:
Calories: 181   Cholesterol: 7 mg
Fat: 4 g   Sodium: 124 mg

CHOCOLATE CREPES

½ cup whole wheat flour
¼ cup unsweetened cocoa powder, sifted
2 tablespoons sugar
¼ teaspoon salt
1 cup nonfat (skim) milk
2 egg whites, lightly beaten

1. Combine the flour and cocoa powder in a bowl. Add the sugar and salt and mix well. Add the milk, slowly beating with a whisk or an egg beater, then stir in the egg whites.

2. Heat a crepe pan until a drop of water dances on the surface. Coat with nonstick vegetable spray and wipe surface with a paper towel. Spoon 2 tablespoons of batter into the pan and tilt the pan from side to side until the batter covers the surface of pan. Cook until edges curl; flip over and cook other side, about 3 minutes total.

3. Keep cooked crepes in a covered container as you make remaining ones. (If you are making them ahead of time or if you plan to freeze the crepes, place pieces of wax paper or aluminum foil between them so they won't stick together. Seal tightly in freezer wrap, Baggies, or an airtight container.)

4. You can serve these crepes as you would pancakes, roll them up for blintzes, or use them with my recipe for Cinnamon-Apple Filling (recipe follows).

MAKES 12 CREPES
Each crepe contains approximately:
Calories: 40   Cholesterol: Negligible
Fat: 1 g   Sodium: 69 mg

CINNAMON-APPLE FILLING

2 tablespoons corn oil margarine
½ cup packed dark brown sugar
¼ cup ground cinnamon
2 pounds golden Delicious apples,
   peeled, cored, and thinly sliced
1 tablespoon vanilla extract
¼ cup fresh lemon juice

Melt the margarine in a large pan. Add the brown sugar and cinnamon, and mix well. Add the apples and cook until they start to soften. Add the vanilla and lemon juice, and cook until apples are very soft. The total cooking time should not exceed 10 minutes. Set aside to cool.

**MAKES 3 CUPS;
TWELVE ¼-CUP SERVINGS**

Each serving contains approximately:
*Calories: 103   Cholesterol: 0 mg
Fat: 2 g   Sodium: 29 mg*

For added color I've garnished the crepes with strips of orange peel and slices of strawberry and kiwi.

VANILLA CREAM SPREAD

1 cup low-fat ricotta cheese
2 tablespoons sugar
1 teaspoon vanilla extract

Combine the ingredients in a food processor with a metal blade and blend until *satin* smooth. Store in the refrigerator.

**MAKES ¾ CUP; TWELVE 1-TABLESPOON
SERVINGS**

Each serving contains approximately:
*Calories: 38   Cholesterol: 6 mg
Fat: 2 g   Sodium: 26 mg*

HEART-HEALTHY CHOCOLATE MUFFINS

2½ cups oat bran

⅓ cup unsweetened cocoa powder, sifted

⅓ cup sugar

1 teaspoon baking soda

½ teaspoon salt

1 teaspoon ground cinnamon

3 egg whites, lightly beaten

2 teaspoons vanilla extract

2 tablespoons canola or corn oil

1¼ cups buttermilk

1 cup fresh or frozen raspberries

1. Preheat the oven to 400°F. Coat a standard (¼-cup) muffin tin with nonstick vegetable spray.

2. Combine the oat bran, cocoa, sugar, baking soda, salt, and cinnamon in a large bowl and mix well.

3. In another bowl combine the egg whites, vanilla, oil, and buttermilk and mix well. Pour the liquid mixture into the dry mixture. Add the raspberries and mix until just moist. *Do not overmix!*

4. Spoon the batter into the prepared tin and bake for 17 minutes.

NOTE: Batter can also be poured into a prepared small muffin tin (2-tablespoon) and baked for 12 minutes.

MAKES 12 LARGE MUFFINS OR 24 SMALL MUFFINS

Each large muffin or 2 small muffins contains approximately:

Calories: 129   Cholesterol: 1 mg

Fat: 5 g   Sodium: 208 mg

CHOCOLATE BREAD

Chocolate Bread is also a fun after-school snack, toasted and spread with peanut butter, as well as a real treat for school lunches.

⅓ cup nonfat (skim) milk

2 tablespoons corn oil margarine

½ cup sugar

⅓ cup cold water

1 envelope (1 tablespoon) active dry yeast (check date on package before using)

2 egg whites, lightly beaten

½ cup unsweetened cocoa powder, sifted

¼ teaspoon salt

1 teaspoon ground cinnamon

1 tablespoon vanilla extract

2½ cups whole wheat flour

1. Scald the milk. Remove from heat and add the margarine and 1 tablespoon of the sugar. Stir until margarine melts. Add cold water and mix well. Pour over yeast and set aside until yeast mixture starts to bubble, about 10 minutes.

2. Combine the egg whites, yeast mixture, remaining sugar, cocoa, salt, cinnamon, and vanilla in a large bowl; mix well. Add the flour, a little at a time, and mix until well blended and the dough forms a ball. Knead in any remaining flour with your hands.

3. Lightly flour the bowl and place the dough ball back in. Cover the bowl with a damp towel and allow dough to rise in a warm place until doubled in bulk, about 1 hour.

4. Punch the dough down and form into a round loaf. Place on an ungreased baking sheet, or form into a rectangular loaf and place in a 9 x 5-inch loaf pan. Preheat the oven to 350°F. Bake loaf for 45 minutes or until it sounds hollow when tapped.

MAKES 1 LOAF; 16 SLICES

Each slice contains approximately:

Calories: 114 *Cholesterol: Negligible*

Fat: 2 g *Sodium: 66 mg*

CHOCOLATE FRENCH TOAST

4 egg whites

1 cup nonfat (skim) milk

¼ teaspoon salt

2 tablespoons maple syrup

8 slices (½ loaf) Chocolate Bread
(previous recipe)

1. Combine the egg whites, milk, salt, and syrup; mix well.

2. Arrange the bread slices in a flat baking dish and pour the liquid over them. Allow to absorb.

3. Heat a large skillet and coat with nonstick vegetable spray. When skillet is hot enough that drops of water dance on the surface, add the bread slices and cook until lightly browned. Turn bread over and lightly brown other side—about 6 minutes total cooking time.

MAKES 8 SLICES

Each slice contains approximately:

Calories: 145 *Cholesterol: 1 mg*

Fat: 2 g *Sodium: 182 mg*

CHOCOLATE BREAD PUDDING WITH CARAMEL SAUCE

¾ loaf Chocolate Bread (page 54), cut in
1-inch cubes (6 cups) (allow to dry
several hours or overnight)

⅓ cup raisins

4 egg whites

¼ cup frozen unsweetened apple juice
concentrate, undiluted

3 tablespoons dark molasses

1½ cups low-fat milk

½ cup canned evaporated skim milk

1½ teaspoons ground cinnamon

1 tablespoon vanilla extract

1½ cups warm Caramel Sauce (recipe
follows)

1. Preheat the oven to 325°F. Combine the bread cubes and raisins in a large mixing bowl and set aside.

2. In large bowl, beat egg whites until frothy. Blend in all remaining ingredients except bread and raisins, and mix well. Pour liquid over bread and raisins and mix well.

3. Coat an 8-inch square baking pan with nonstick vegetable spray. Spoon the bread mixture into the pan and pat down evenly. Bake for 50 minutes or until a knife inserted in center comes out clean. If the top starts to brown too much, cover with aluminum foil.

4. Remove pudding from oven and allow to cool slightly before cutting into sixteen 2-inch squares. Cut each square into 3 slices and top each 3-slice serving with 1½ tablespoons of warm sauce.

MAKES 16 SERVINGS

Each serving (with sauce) contains approximately:

Calories: 185 *Cholesterol: 3 mg*

Fat: 4 g *Sodium: 120 mg*

Chocolate Bread Pudding with Caramel Sauce.

CARAMEL SAUCE

1¼ cups 2% low-fat milk
1 tablespoon cornstarch
2 tablespoons corn-oil margarine
½ cup packed dark brown sugar
1 teaspoon vanilla extract

1. Combine the milk and cornstarch in a small saucepan and mix until cornstarch is thoroughly dissolved. Add the margarine and brown sugar and cook over medium heat, stirring constantly with a wire whisk, until mixture thickens and comes to a boil. Continue to boil for 1 minute.

2. Remove pan from the heat and stir in the vanilla. Serve warm.

MAKES 1½ CUPS SAUCE; SIXTEEN 1½ TABLESPOON SERVINGS
Each serving contains approximately:
Calories: 51   Cholesterol: 1 mg
Fat: 2 g   Sodium: 31 mg

CREAMY VANILLA SAUCE

2 cups low-fat ricotta cheese
⅓ cup plain nonfat yogurt
⅓ cup sugar
1 tablespoon vanilla extract

Combine the ingredients in a food processor with a metal blade and blend until *satin* smooth. This sauce is wonderful on fruit, toast, pancakes, waffles, or as a cereal topping.

MAKES 1½ CUPS; TWENTY-FOUR 1-TABLESPOON SERVINGS
Each serving contains approximately:
Calories: 42   Cholesterol: 6 mg
Fat: 2 g   Sodium: 28 mg

CHOCOLATE SAUCE

1½ cups nonfat (skim) milk
2 tablespoons corn oil margarine
½ cup unsweetened cocoa powder, sifted
½ cup sugar
½ teaspoon ground cinnamon
1 teaspoon vanilla extract

1. Pour the milk into a saucepan and bring to a boil.

2. Melt the margarine in another saucepan. Add the cocoa and cook over low heat for 3 minutes, stirring constantly. *Do not burn!* Pour hot milk into cocoa mixture, stirring constantly with a wire whisk. Add the sugar and cinnamon, and continue to simmer, stirring constantly until thickened. Remove from heat, add vanilla, and mix well. This sauce is good served hot, at room temperature, or cold on ice cream, yogurt, pancakes, poached fruit—use your imagination!

**MAKES 1½ CUPS; TWENTY-FOUR
1-TABLESPOON SERVINGS**
Each serving contains approximately:
Calories: 36   Cholesterol: Negligible
Fat: 1 g   Sodium: 21 mg

FRESH BERRY SAUCE

¾ pound fresh or thawed frozen
    raspberries, pureed
¾ pound fresh or thawed frozen
    strawberries
2 tablespoons sugar

Strain the raspberries to remove seeds; then combine the puree with the strawberries and sugar in a bowl and mix well. This sauce is delicious as a jam on toast, pancakes, or waffles. It is also a wonderful topping for ice cream, yogurt, and cereal.

**MAKES 1½ CUPS; TWENTY-FOUR
1-TABLESPOON SERVINGS**
Each serving contains approximately:
Calories: 15   Cholesterol: 0 mg
Fat: Negligible   Sodium: Negligible

A trio of sauces with Chocolate Crepes.

LUNCH

In many cultures lunch is the biggest and most important meal of the day. For some, however, it is simply a make-do meal eaten in a hurry and without much concern for the quality of the food. But lunch can be fun, even the most desirable time to entertain family and friends.

Because lunch is a neglected opportunity to entertain, you may discover many people are available and on shorter notice than if you were trying to plan a dinner party. There are people who don't like to eat large meals at night or who plan evening events that interfere with other family activities. While it might be less convenient to have children as dinner guests, especially if the hour is late, they can often be included in a luncheon.

Whatever your reasons for midday entertaining, here are luncheon menus that can be used in total or in part, depending on your preferences and the purpose of the event. Of course, all the menus can be adapted for your dinner parties. You will see that the possibilities are endless.

Best of the Southwest

❖

Tortilla Soup

Confetti Salad

Soft Prawn Tacos with
Papaya Salsa

Chocolate Bread Pudding
with Caramel-Rum Sauce

This is an exciting and popular theme menu that works well for all occasions. When using this for a birthday party, serve the Chocolate Bread Pudding on a large plate, pour the sauce over the top, and decorate it with colorful candles.

TORTILLA SOUP

This is one of my favorite soups. Not only is it a marvelous first course, but it is also perfect served with quesadillas for a South-western "soup and sandwich" lunch. If you like a bit more bite to your soup, add a touch more cayenne pepper or a few drops of Tabasco.

6 *corn tortillas*

6 *garlic cloves*

2 *tablespoons chopped cilantro (fresh coriander)*

2 *quarts (8 cups) defatted Chicken Stock (page 40)*

1 *large onion, chopped*

2 *pounds plum tomatoes, peeled, or a 2-pound can, drained*

2 *teaspoons ground cumin*

2 *teaspoons chili powder*

2 *bay leaves, crumbled*

½ *teaspoon salt (omit if using salted stock)*

⅛ *teaspoon cayenne pepper*

1½ *cups julienned cooked chicken breast (9 ounces raw)*

¾ *cup (3 ounces) grated 20% fat-reduced Monterey Jack cheese*
Cilantro sprigs, for garnish (optional)

1. Preheat the oven to 350°F. Cut 3 of the tortillas in thin strips and place them on a nonstick baking sheet. Bake until crisp and a rich, golden brown, about 15 minutes (watch carefully as they burn easily). Set aside. (This is also a great way to make your own healthy tortilla chips for snacking.)

2. Chop the remaining tortillas coarsely and put them in a large, heavy saucepan. Add the garlic, cilantro, and 2 cups of chicken stock. Bring to a boil, reduce heat, and simmer until tortillas are soft.

3. Combine the chopped onion and 1 cup of the chicken stock in a blender and puree. Pour the pureed onion into the pan with the tortillas. Put the tomatoes into a blender and puree, then add to the saucepan. Mix well and continue to simmer. Add the cumin, chili powder, bay leaves, salt, and cayenne pepper. Add all the remaining stock and bring to a boil. Reduce heat and simmer, uncovered, for 30 minutes, stirring frequently.

4. Strain the soup and pour into warm bowls. To each bowl add ¼ cup of cooked chicken strips and 2 tablespoons of grated cheese. Garnish with toasted tortilla strips and cilantro sprigs, or serve the strips in a separate dish and allow your guests to add them to their own soup.

MAKES SIX 1-CUP SERVINGS
Each serving contains approximately:

Calories: 255   Cholesterol: 36 mg

Fat: 7 g   Sodium: 415 mg

61

CONFETTI SALAD

The minute you take a bite you'll love the combination of tastes and textures in this salad. Even if you hate dicing vegetables, you'll be anxious to make it again. I sometimes add diced, cooked chicken and serve the salad as an entree.

½ jicama, peeled

½ red bell pepper, seeds and membranes removed

½ yellow bell pepper, seeds and membranes removed

1 zucchini

1 carrot, peeled

DRESSING

¼ cup fresh lime juice

¼ teaspoon salt

¼ teaspoon cayenne pepper

2 tablespoons peanut oil

2 tablespoons rice vinegar

2 tablespoons honey

2 heads Belgian endive, separated into leaves

2 tablespoons coarsely chopped dry-roasted peanuts

1. Dice all the vegetables in ¼-inch cubes and place in a bowl.

2. In another bowl, combine the lime juice and salt. Stir until salt is completely dissolved, then add remaining dressing ingredients and mix well. (Makes ½ cup dressing.) Add dressing to diced vegetables and mix well.

3. Line 6 chilled salad plates with 2 or 3 Belgian endive leaves. Arrange ⅔ cup of the salad on each plate. Top each serving with 1 teaspoon of chopped peanuts.

MAKES SIX ⅔-CUP SERVINGS

Each serving contains approximately:

Calories: 106   Cholesterol: 0 mg

Fat: 6 g   Sodium: 105 mg

O P P O S I T E : Soft Prawn Tacos with Papaya Salsa.

SOFT PRAWN TACOS
WITH PAPAYA SALSA

The inspiration for these tacos came from the lobster tacos on Dean Fearing's menu at The Mansion, in Dallas. This idea also works for other seafood and poultry as well. I like this version best because of the look of the tacos topped with butterflied prawns.

> 6 whole wheat tortillas
> 1 pound fresh prawns or shrimp, peeled and deveined but tails attached
> ¼ cup defatted Chicken Stock (page 40)
> ¾ cup grated jalapeño Jack cheese
> 1½ cups shredded spinach leaves
> 3 cups Papaya Salsa (recipe follows)

1. Preheat the oven to 300°F. Wrap the tortillas lightly in aluminum foil and warm in oven for 15 minutes.

2. Select the 6 largest prawns and set aside. Remove tails from the remaining prawns and dice the prawns. Bring chicken stock to a boil in a sauté pan, add the diced prawns, and cook just until they turn from translucent to opaque, about 1 minute. *Do not overcook.*

3. Remove prawns from stock and set aside. Leaving tails attached to remaining 6 prawns, butterfly them by cutting them in half lengthwise up the back (vein side) to within 1 inch of the tail. Bring the stock back to a boil and cook the butterflied prawns until they turn from translucent to opaque, about 1 minute. Reserve butterflied prawns for garnish.

4. Remove warm tortillas from foil and spoon equal amounts of diced prawns down the center of each. Sprinkle 2 tablespoons grated cheese evenly over the prawns in each taco. Top with ¼ cup shredded spinach. Roll tortilla into a cylinder-shape and place, seam side up, on a large warm plate. Top each taco with 1 butterflied prawn. Spoon ¼ cup of salsa on each side of the tacos and serve.

MAKES 6 SERVINGS
Each serving contains approximately:
Calories: 345   *Cholesterol: 140 mg*
Fat: 14 g   *Sodium: 349 mg*

PAPAYA SALSA

This tropical salsa is the perfect accompaniment for the tacos. I also like it on broiled fish and poultry. If ripe papayas are not available, use a mango, peaches, or a melon.

> 2 papayas (2 pounds) peeled and finely diced (3 cups)
> 1 shallot, minced (1 tablespoon)
> 1 garlic clove, minced (1 teaspoon)
> 2 tablespoons tightly packed minced cilantro (fresh coriander)
> ¼ cup canned green chilies, chopped
> 1 tablespoon rice vinegar
> 2 teaspoons fresh lime juice

Combine the ingredients and mix well. Cover and refrigerate for several hours before serving.

MAKES 3 CUPS; SIX ½-CUP SERVINGS
Each serving contains approximately:
Calories: 32   *Cholesterol: 0 mg*
Fat: Negligible   *Sodium: 70 mg*

CHOCOLATE BREAD PUDDING
WITH CARAMEL-RUM SAUCE

The only difference between this pudding and the one that graced our opulent Ultimate Chocolate Fantasy brunch is a touch of rum in the sauce, which adds just the right finishing flavor to this menu.

> 6 squares Chocolate Bread Pudding (page 55)
> 9 tablespoons Caramel Sauce (page 56)
> 1 teaspoon Myer's dark rum

To serve, slice each square of pudding into thirds and layer them on the plate. Combine the sauce and rum, then spoon 1½ tablespoons of sauce over each serving.

MAKES 6 SERVINGS
Each serving contains approximately:
Calories: 187   *Cholesterol: 2 mg*
Fat: 2 g   *Sodium: 89 mg*

Serving champagne with the Chocolate Bread Pudding ends the meal on a festive note.

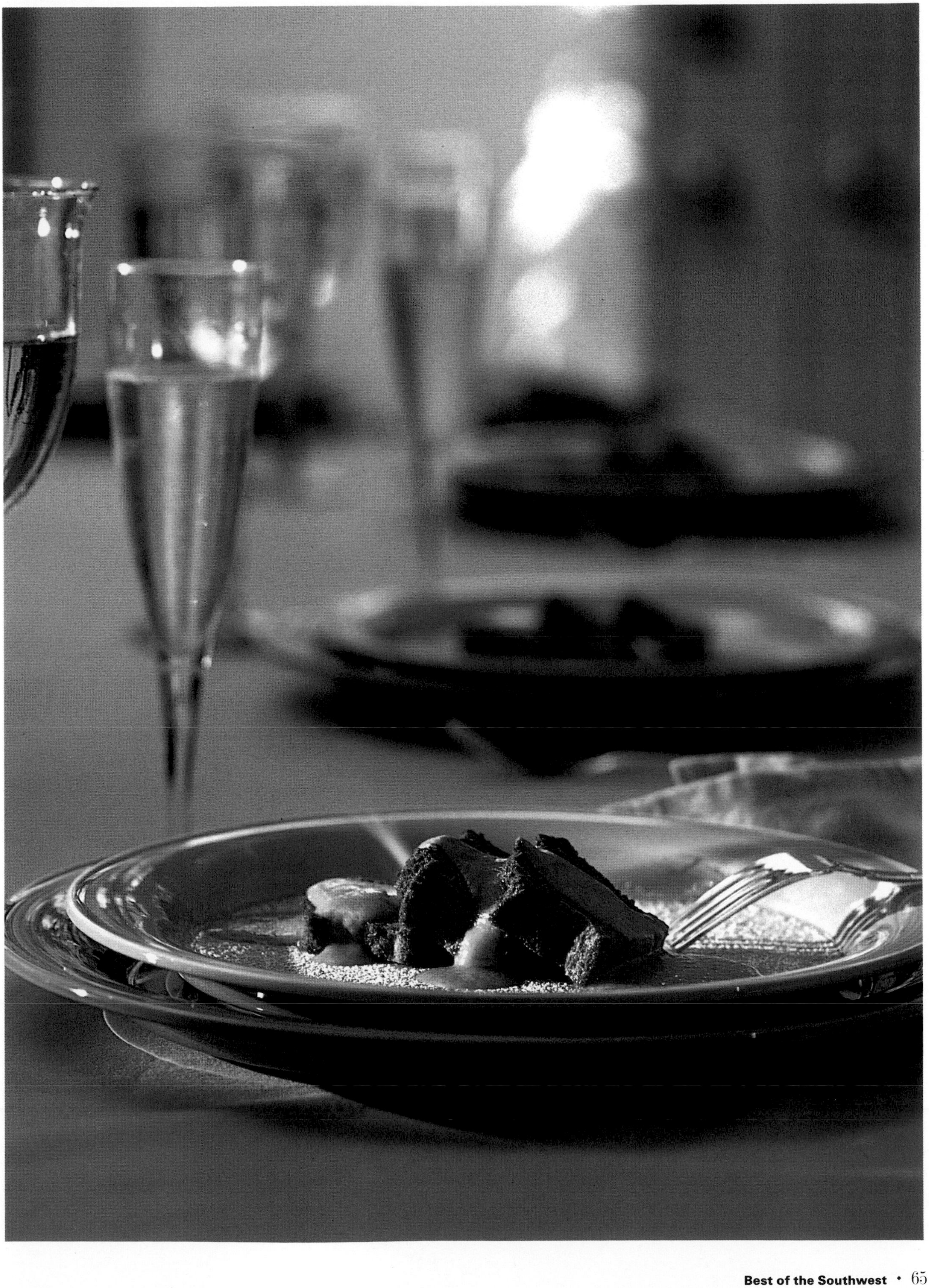

Bridge Luncheon

❖

Curried Fruit Soup

Oriental Pasta and Chicken Salad

Frozen Key Lime Cloud

When it's your turn to host the bridge club, plan ahead. This menu allows you time to play the game, enjoy your own lunch, and impress your bridge group, all at the same time. As perfect as this lunch is for a bridge get-together, it is not limited to the bridge table. The menu adapts well to buffet service and would work well for a birthday party, bridal shower, or any other occasion when you want a completely make-ahead meal.

CURRIED FRUIT SOUP

The secret to a flavorful success with this fruit soup is to make it up to the point where you add the bananas the day before you plan to serve it. The flavors marry and the soup has more character.

> 1 16-ounce can water-packed peaches, including liquid
> 1 8-ounce can juice-packed crushed pineapple, including juice
> 2 teaspoons curry powder
> ⅛ teaspoon ground ginger
> Dash of salt
> 2 tablespoons brandy
> 1 banana, sliced (1 cup)

> 3 tablespoons frozen unsweetened apple juice concentrate, undiluted
> ¼ teaspoon fresh lemon juice
> ¼ cup plain nonfat yogurt
> 4 mint leaves, for garnish (optional)

1. The day before serving, drain the peaches and pour the liquid into a saucepan. Chop the peaches and add to the pan along with the pineapple and juice. Add the curry powder, ginger, and salt. Mix well and bring to a boil. Reduce the heat to low and simmer, uncovered, for 15 minutes.

2. Add the brandy and simmer for 10 more minutes. Cool to room temperature, cover, and refrigerate for at least 12 hours.

3. To serve, pour the fruit mixture into a blender container. Add the banana, apple juice concentrate, and lemon juice; blend until soup is *satin* smooth.

4. Pour mixture into a saucepan and heat to desired temperature, then pour ¾ cup in each of 4 bowls. Top each serving with 1 tablespoon yogurt and a mint leaf.

MAKES FOUR ¾-CUP SERVINGS
Each serving contains approximately:
Calories: 140   *Cholesterol: Negligible*
Fat: Negligible   *Sodium: 60 mg*

ORIENTAL PASTA AND CHICKEN SALAD

This is my all-time favorite pasta salad. I love the combination of tastes and textures. I also love the fact that I can make it the night before and have it taste even better. I have used chicken breast here, but it is also good made with water-packed tuna. If you can't find Mongolian Fire Oil, any hot pepper oil will do.

¼ cup chopped raw almonds

DRESSING

¼ cup frozen unsweetened apple juice concentrate, undiluted

¼ cup rice vinegar

1½ tablespoons dark sesame oil

½ teaspoon peeled fresh ginger, minced

½ teaspoon salt

½ teaspoon freshly ground black pepper

½ garlic clove, minced

½ teaspoon Mongolian Fire Oil (available in Oriental markets)

SALAD

2 whole chicken breasts, boned and skinned

6 cups water

4 ounces (½ package) instant Chuka Soba noodles (available in Oriental markets)

½ head green cabbage, thinly sliced (6 cups)

4 green onions, chopped (1 cup)

4 green onion tops, for garnish (optional)

1. Preheat the oven to 350°F. Toast the almonds for 8 to 10 minutes or until golden brown. Watch carefully; they burn easily. Set aside. Keep oven on.

2. Combine the dressing ingredients; mix well and set aside.

3. Bake the chicken, covered, in 350°F. oven for 15 minutes. Remove from oven, leave covered, and allow to cool for 20 minutes. Cut chicken into thin strips and, if not using immediately, cover tightly with plastic wrap and refrigerate until needed.

4. Bring the water to a boil. Add noodles and cook, stirring, for 2 to 3 minutes. Drain thoroughly, then place in a bowl, add dressing, and toss thoroughly. Add the cabbage and chopped green onions, and again mix thoroughly. Add the chicken; mix well. Cover and refrigerate, stirring occasionally, for at least 4 hours or overnight if desired.

5. To serve, place 1½ cups of salad on each of 4 chilled plates. Top each serving with 1 tablespoon toasted almonds and a green onion top.

MAKES FOUR 1½-CUP SERVINGS

Each serving contains approximately:

Calories: 445   Cholesterol: 72 mg

Fat: 14 g   Sodium: 408 mg

FROZEN KEY LIME CLOUD

This tangy dessert is indeed a heavenly treat. I often garnish it with orange zest instead of lime for a bit more color. If you are making a larger quantity for a buffet-style luncheon, you may want to freeze it in one large dish and scoop out individual servings onto plates instead of using individual bowls or goblets.

> 2 egg whites
> ½ cup instant nonfat dry milk powder
> ½ cup water
> 1 egg yolk, lightly beaten
> ¼ cup sugar
> ¼ teaspoon finely grated lime peel
> 3 tablespoons fresh lime juice

1. Combine the egg whites, powdered milk, and water in a bowl and beat, using an electric mixer, until stiff peaks form.

2. In another bowl, combine the egg yolk, sugar, lime peel, and lime juice. Mix well and slowly add to the whipped mixture while continuing to beat.

3. Spoon 1 cup of the cloud carefully into each of 4 chilled bowls. Place in freezer until frozen (about 2 hours) and then garnish before serving.

MAKES 4 SERVINGS

Each serving contains approximately:

Calories: 106   Cholesterol: 55 mg

Fat: 1 g   Sodium: 76 mg

Sometimes I wait until the first few hands have been played to serve dessert.

Midday in the Midwest

❖

Bibb Lettuce Salad with
Thousand Island Dressing

Meatloaf

Mashed Potatoes with
Country Gravy

Herbed Brussels Sprouts

Cherry-Rhubarb Trifle

Here is a hearty, heartland menu perfect for a weekend get-together of family or friends. Designed to be served family style, this menu is also good served buffet or in courses.

For a family meal, iced tea is a nice alternative to wine.

BIBB LETTUCE SALAD WITH THOUSAND ISLAND DRESSING

❖

This salad is my '90s update of the wedge of iceberg lettuce. The thousand island dressing will surprise your guests, for it is a tasty dressing with only a fraction of the calories found in the traditional recipe. Combining the tofu with lemon juice and just a tiny bit of canola or corn oil gives it a mayonnaiselike quality without the fat and cholesterol. The rest of the ingredients indeed capture the flavor of a splendid and classic thousand island dressing.

> *8 small heads Bibb lettuce*
> *1 cup Thousand Island Dressing (recipe*
> *follows)*

1. Wash the lettuce, leaving the heads intact. Turn upside down on paper or cloth towels and allow to drain thoroughly.

2. To serve, place each head on a salad plate and top each with 2 tablespoons of dressing.

MAKES 8 SERVINGS

Each serving (with dressing) contains approximately:

Calories: 24	*Cholesterol: 0 mg*
Fat: 1 g	*Sodium: 67 mg*

Thousand Island Dressing

1 cup silken soft tofu
½ cup bottled chili sauce
2 tablespoons red wine vinegar
1½ teaspoons canola or corn oil
1½ teaspoons fresh lemon juice
¾ teaspoon sugar
¼ teaspoon salt
¼ teaspoon freshly ground black pepper
¼ cup sweet pickle relish

1. Combine all ingredients except pickle relish in a blender container and blend until smooth. Pour dressing into a bowl, add pickle relish, and mix well.

2. Store covered in refrigerator.

**MAKES 2 CUPS;
SIXTEEN 2-TABLESPOON SERVINGS**
Each serving contains approximately:
Calories: 23   Cholesterol: 0 mg
Fat: 1 g   Sodium: 67 mg

MEATLOAF

Everyone has a favorite meatloaf recipe and here is mine. This is a revision of Chef Henry Haller's famous Whitehouse Meatloaf, which I revised for my column several years ago. Use the tomato paste topping off the meatloaf to spread on bread for meatloaf sandwiches the next day.

> 1 cup finely chopped onion
> 2 garlic cloves, minced
> 3 slices whole wheat bread
> 1 cup nonfat (skim) milk
> 2 pounds very lean ground beef
> 3 egg whites, lightly beaten
> 1 teaspoon salt
> ¼ teaspoon freshly ground black pepper
> ¼ cup finely chopped fresh parsley
> ¾ teaspoon dried thyme leaves, crushed
>   with mortar and pestle
> ¾ teaspoon dried marjoram, crushed
>   with a mortar and pestle
> 1 6-ounce can tomato paste

1. Place the onion and garlic in a nonstick or cast iron skillet and cook covered over very low heat, stirring occasionally, for about 20 minutes or until soft. Uncover and cook over medium heat until golden brown, about 3 more minutes.

2. Remove the crusts from the bread. Place crusts in a blender jar or food processor and blend to make fine bread crumbs. Set aside. Dice the remaining bread into ½-inch cubes and soak in milk.

3. In a large mixing bowl, mix the beef by hand with the sautéed onion and garlic and the bread cubes. Add the egg whites, salt, pepper, parsley, thyme, and marjoram, and mix by hand in a circular motion.

4. Coat a wire rack with nonstick vegetable spray and place in baking dish. Pat meat into a loaf shape and place on rack. There should be at least 1 inch of space between the loaf and the edge of the baking dish to catch splatters and allow fat to drain off. (If you don't have a rack that will fit your baking dish, use a broiler pan with a slotted top.) Refrigerate for 1 hour to allow the flavors to blend and to firm up the loaf.

5. Preheat the oven to 375°F. Bake meatloaf on the lower shelf of the oven for 30 minutes. Remove from oven and spread with tomato paste and sprinkle with reserved bread crumbs. Return to oven and cook an additional 30 minutes. Pour off accumulated fat after meat is fully cooked. Let stand for 5 minutes before slicing.

MAKES 8 SERVINGS

Each serving contains approximately:

Calories: 303   *Cholesterol: 87 mg*

Fat: 16 g   *Sodium: 622 mg*

MASHED POTATOES

The trick to yummy, fluffy mashed potatoes is beating them with an electric mixer to double their volume. The texture is much lighter and you get twice as much for the same number of calories!

> 2 pounds baking potatoes, peeled and
>   chopped
> 2 tablespoons corn oil margarine, melted
> ⅛ teaspoon salt
> ⅛ teaspoon freshly ground black pepper
> ¾ cup nonfat (skim) milk

1. Boil potatoes until tender. Drain. With a potato masher, mash while they are still hot until all lumps disappear.

2. Add the melted margarine, salt, pepper, and milk to the potatoes and beat with an electric mixer until doubled in volume.

3. Serve hot.

MAKES EIGHT ½-CUP SERVINGS

Each serving contains approximately:

Calories: 102   *Cholesterol: Negligible*

Fat: 3 g   *Sodium: 92 mg*

Meatloaf makes a comeback.

Country Gravy

◆

Country Gravy is the new light gravy to replace all those calorie- and fat-laden ones you may still have in your recipe file. It has all of the flavor of more traditional gravies but is much more considerate of your waistline and arteries.

When roasting a turkey or chicken, save the drippings from the roasting pan and place in the freezer or refrigerator until the fat congeals on the top and can be removed easily. Then store in the freezer until you need it to make sauces and gravies. Otherwise you can proceed as in this recipe by reducing stock to intensify its flavor.

> 4 cups defatted turkey or Chicken Stock (page 40)
>
> 3 tablespoons cornstarch
>
> ¼ cup water
>
> 1 teaspoon corn oil margarine
>
> ¼ pound fresh mushrooms, washed and sliced (1 cup)
>
> Salt and pepper to taste

1. In a saucepan over medium heat, cook the stock until reduced in volume by one-third. (If using 2 cups drippings, this step isn't necessary because the drippings will already have the intensity of flavor that the reduced stock will achieve. Simply heat the drippings to a simmer and proceed.) When reduced, dissolve the cornstarch in the water and slowly add to simmering mixture, stirring constantly. Cook slowly, stirring occasionally, until mixture returns to a simmer and thickens slightly to desired consistency.

2. In a skillet over medium heat, melt the margarine. Add the mushrooms and cook until tender, about 5 minutes. Add to gravy and season with salt and pepper.

MAKES EIGHT ⅓-CUP SERVINGS

Each serving contains approximately:

Calories: 33   Cholesterol: Negligible

Fat: 1 g   Sodium: 45 mg

N O T E : If you refrigerate this gravy the cornstarch will break down, leaving the gravy a watery mess. To solve this problem just bring the gravy back to a boil, dissolve a little more cornstarch in cold water, and add it to the gravy to thicken it again.

Herbed Brussels Sprouts

◆

> 2 pounds Brussels sprouts
>
> 2 tablespoons canola or corn oil
>
> ¼ teaspoon salt
>
> 1 tablespoon minced fresh basil, or 1 teaspoon dried, crushed with a mortar and pestle
>
> ¼ cup minced fresh parsley
>
> ¼ cup minced chives or green onion tops

Steam the Brussels sprouts until just crisp-tender, about 8 to 10 minutes. Heat the oil, add all the other ingredients, and cook for 5 minutes over low heat. Add the cooked sprouts and mix thoroughly.

N O T E : If you are making this dish ahead of time, run cold water over the cooked sprouts to keep them green. Then reheat them in the herb sauce, being careful not to overcook them.

MAKES 8 1-CUP SERVINGS

Each serving contains approximately:

Calories: 80   Cholesterol: 0 mg

Fat: 4 g   Sodium: 101 mg

V A R I A T I O N S : Many other green vegetables are delicious prepared in this manner. I have used Brussels sprouts here because many people who do not particularly care for them love them this way. If you *really* don't like Brussels sprouts, try this with broccoli, asparagus, or thickly sliced zucchini instead.

Cherry-Rhubarb Trifle

Truly the ultimate trifle! This one is beautiful, unusual, delicious, low in calories, and contains practically no cholesterol or saturated fat. The rhubarb adds a wonderful texture and a delightfully different, subtle flavor not usually found in trifles made only with soft fruits.

　　　2 *cups nonfat (skim) milk*
　　　2 *tablespoons cornstarch*
　⅓ *cup sugar*
　　　4 *egg whites, lightly beaten*
　　　2 *teaspoons canola or corn oil*
　1½ *teaspoons vanilla extract*
　　　8 *ounces angel food cake, cut into 1-*
　　　　　inch cubes (4 cups)
　　　6 *tablespoons dry sherry*
　　　1 *pound pitted dark unsweetened frozen*
　　　　　cherries, thawed (2 cups)
　　　8 *ounces rhubarb, diced and steamed (1*
　　　　　cup)

1. Combine the milk and cornstarch in a saucepan and mix until the cornstarch is completely dissolved. Add the sugar, egg whites, and oil; mix well. Slowly bring to a boil, stirring constantly with a wire whisk until thickened. Remove from heat, add vanilla, and allow to cool to room temperature.

2. Assemble the trifle. Place one-third of the cake pieces in the bottom of a 2-quart glass bowl or trifle dish. Sprinkle with 2 tablespoons sherry. Spoon ⅔ cup of the "custard" mixture over the cake. Spoon ⅔ cup cherries over the custard, then ⅓ cup rhubarb. Repeat the process twice. Cover and refrigerate.

3. To serve bring the trifle dish to the table and place in individual bowls or on small plates. You can also make individual trifles.

MAKES TWELVE ½-CUP SERVINGS
Each serving contains approximately:
　Calories: 150　Cholesterol: 1 mg
　Fat: 1 g　　　Sodium: 93 mg

DINNER

At the end of the day, with all of our other activities behind us, it's fun to change gears, relax, and enjoy sharing the evening meal with our families and friends. So it's not surprising that dinner is the most popular meal for entertaining.

In this section I have tried to cover a wide variety of dinner possibilities. Whether you are packing a beach picnic or setting the table for a formal dinner party, the most important rule is to use your imagination and add your own personal touches. Remember, you are always the one giving your party, whether it's for two or two hundred, and it should reflect your own style, taste, and personality.

Portable Sunset Supper

❖

*Tomato and Peppered Cheese
with Balsamic Dressing*

Tuscan Bean and Tuna Salad

Herbed Country Bread

Biscotti d'Anise

This is a perfect picnic menu because it travels so well and can be prepared hours ahead without suffering the consequences. Going directly from work to the beach, the mountains, or simply to a local park, you can literally pack your Sunset Supper in the trunk of your car in the morning and have a relaxed, romantic, *al fresco* dinner for two at the end of the day. This country Italian meal also expands easily to accommodate any size crowd for a larger picnic or a tailgate party.

I pack a small ice chest just for the peppered cheese and wine. I bring the tuna, in the unopened can, and add it to the Tuscan Beans just before serving. This salad is best served at room temperature and fresh tomatoes taste better if they are never refrigerated. Neither the bread nor the biscotti require refrigeration.

Portable beach tables are inexpensive and readily available, and they make dining on the sand more enjoyable.

TOMATO AND PEPPERED CHEESE WITH BALSAMIC DRESSING

The combination of vine-ripened tomatoes with fresh buffalo mozzarella has long been one of my favorite appetizers. This dish captures much of the same flavor and texture and is lower in calories, cholesterol, and saturated fat. I use low-fat ricotta cheese in place of the higher-fat mozzarella, and season it with freshly ground black pepper. The combination of a strongly flavored extra-virgin olive oil and balsamic vinegar adds just the right amount of tanginess and texture. I mold the cheese for this presentation to more closely resemble sliced buffalo mozzarella, however this step can be eliminated.

   ½ cup low-fat ricotta cheese
   ¼ teaspoon freshly ground black pepper
   4 slices ripe tomato

   1 tablespoon extra-virgin olive oil
   1 teaspoon balsamic vinegar
     Fresh basil leaves, for garnish
     (optional)

1. Combine the ricotta cheese and pepper and mix well. Press half of the cheese mixture into a ¼-cup oiled mold and tap to release from mold. Repeat with remaining cheese mixture.

2. Arrange 2 tomato slices and 1 molded cheese on each of 2 plates.

3. Combine the olive oil and vinegar and drizzle 2 teaspoons over each serving. Garnish with fresh basil leaves.

MAKES 2 SERVINGS

Each serving contains approximately:

Calories: 152   Cholesterol: 19 mg

Fat: 12 g   Sodium: 80 mg

TUSCAN BEAN AND TUNA SALAD

The inspiration for this salad came from Lorenza d'Medici's cooking school in Tuscany, Badia a Coltibuono. The two secrets to its success are in serving it at room temperature rather than cold and in using a solid white albacore rather than a softer textured, darker tuna.

> ½ cup dried white beans, soaked
>   overnight
> 1 tablespoon extra-virgin olive oil
> ¼ medium onion, thinly sliced
> 1½ tablespoons fresh lemon juice
> ¼ teaspoon salt
> ¼ teaspoon freshly ground black pepper
> 2 tablespoons chopped fresh basil
> 1 3½-ounce can water-packed white
>   albacore tuna, drained and flaked

1. Drain the beans and put in a saucepan. Cover with water and cook, covered, over low heat for 1½ hours. Drain well and mix with olive oil. Set aside.

2. Soak the sliced onion in cold water for 30 minutes; drain thoroughly and set aside. Combine the lemon juice and salt, and mix until salt is completely dissolved; add pepper and mix well. Add the beans, onion, and basil and mix well. Just before serving, add the tuna and mix well. Serve at room temperature.

MAKES TWO 1¼-CUP SERVINGS
Each serving contains approximately:
Calories: 396   Cholesterol: 9 mg
Fat: 8 g   Sodium: 484 mg

Tuscan Bean and Tuna Salad with Herbed Country Bread.

HERBED COUNTRY BREAD

This country bread is my own favorite, both to make and to eat. It requires practically no kneading and no second rise so it is, therefore, very easy and quick to make. It has a wonderful, rough texture—which I love—and a robust, satisfying flavor. It goes well with this menu, but I also like to serve it as an appetizer with the eggplant filling-sauce from my Marinated Eggplant Antipasto (page 94) as a dip. For people who don't like to make yeast breads, I have also included this nonyeast, quick bread, which is also delicious.

> ⅔ cup cool water
> 2 teaspoons sugar
> ⅔ cup nonfat (skim) milk
> 2 envelopes (2 tablespoons) active dry
>   yeast (check date on package before
>   using)
> 3 egg whites, lightly beaten
> 1 teaspoon salt
> ¾ teaspoon rosemary, crushed with a
>   mortar and pestle
> ¼ teaspoon thyme, crushed with a mortar
>   and pestle
> 3 tablespoons extra-virgin olive oil
> 4 cups whole wheat flour
>   Oat bran

1. Bring the water to a boil. Remove from the heat, add the sugar and milk, and mix well. When this mixture is warm to the touch, but not hot (too much heat will kill the yeast), add the yeast, mix well, and set aside until yeast starts to bubble, about 10 minutes.

2. Combine the egg whites, salt, rosemary, thyme, and olive oil. Add the yeast mixture and mix well. Add the flour, a little at a time, mixing well after each addition. Knead into a ball and place, covered, in a warm place to rise until doubled in bulk, about 1 hour.

3. Preheat the oven to 350°F. Punch dough down, knead into a ball, and roll in oat bran. Press the ball of dough flat, forming a large circle. Sprinkle more oat bran on a baking sheet and place the bread dough on the oat bran. Bake for 35 minutes, or until lightly browned. Let cool, then cut into wedges and serve.

MAKES 32 PIE-SHAPED WEDGES
Each slice contains approximately:
Calories: 70   Cholesterol: Negligible
Fat: 2 g   Sodium: 82 mg

QUICK HERB BREAD

1 cup whole wheat flour
1 cup unbleached all-purpose flour
1 tablespoon baking powder
½ teaspoon baking soda
4 teaspoons sugar
4 tablespoons (½ stick) corn oil
    margarine, chilled
⅔ cup buttermilk
1 egg, lightly beaten
½ teaspoon dried rosemary, crushed with
    a mortar and pestle
¼ teaspoon dried thyme, crushed with a
    mortar and pestle
Buttermilk, for glazing

1. Preheat oven to 325°F. Combine flours, baking powder, baking soda, and sugar in a large mixing bowl and mix well. Add margarine and, using a pastry blender, blend mixture until it is the consistency of coarse cornmeal.

2. Combine buttermilk and egg and add to dry ingredients. Add herbs and mix well. Remove dough to a floured board and knead in more flour to make dough smooth and elastic.

3. Coat an 8-inch round pan with nonstick vegetable spray. Place dough in pan and press it down so dough fills entire pan. Cut a deep crease in top of bread so sides will not crack while baking. Brush top lightly with buttermilk and bake for 35 to 40 minutes, or until a light golden brown. Remove from the oven and let cool on rack to room temperature. The loaf is much easier to slice when cool. If you wish to serve the bread hot, slice it, wrap it in foil, and reheat in the oven.

MAKES SIXTEEN 1-SLICE SERVINGS
Each serving contains approximately:
Calories: 91   Cholesterol: 14 mg
Fat: 4 g   Sodium: 205 mg

BISCOTTI D'ANISE

I try to keep these on hand in my kitchen at all times. This wonderfully crunchy Italian cookie is sort of a crisp, more flavorful ladyfinger. I serve them with morning coffee, afternoon tea, and fresh fruit for dessert.

2 tablespoons corn oil margarine
½ cup sugar
4 egg whites, lightly beaten
1 teaspoon vanilla extract
2 cups unbleached all-purpose flour
1 teaspoon baking powder
¼ teaspoon salt
2 teaspoons ground anise seeds
2 teaspoons lemon zest

1. Preheat the oven to 375°F. Combine the margarine and sugar and mix until fluffy. Add the egg whites and vanilla. Mix well.

2. In another bowl, combine the flour, baking powder, salt, anise seeds, and lemon zest; mix well. Add to other ingredients and mix well.

3. Roll dough into 24 small cigar-shape cookies, each about 3 inches long, and place on a baking sheet that has been coated with nonstick vegetable spray. Bake for 15 minutes. Remove from oven and reduce oven temperature to 325°F.

4. While cookies are still warm, cut in half lengthwise. Place on cookie sheet cut side up, and return to oven for 15 more minutes. Cool completely and store in an airtight container.

MAKES 48 BISCOTTI
Each biscotti contains approximately:
Calories: 32   Cholesterol: 0 mg
Fat: 1 g   Sodium: 37 mg

Grapes are perfect for a picnic since they require no preparation.

A Taste of Asia

❖

Thai-Type Soup

Chinese Firecracker Salad with
Thai Peanut Dressing

Seafood Potstickers

Pork Tenderloin in Teriyaki-Pear Sauce

Chuka Soba Noodles

Stir-Fried Sesame Asparagus

Sticky Black Rice Pudding

I have incorporated a few of my favorite Asian recipes into this menu. Each complements the other in a delightful way. I use a dining room setting for this meal because I feature an antique Japanese *obi* given to me by one of my guests. This menu is also fun to serve on low tables in your living room, seating your guests on cushions on the floor.

O P P O S I T E : I've chosen two traditional Asian beverages to serve with this meal: hot tea and warm sake. **R I G H T :** Thai-Type Soup.

THAI-TYPE SOUP

This soup is an imposter. The real Thai recipe calls for fresh lemongrass. which is very difficult to find. and coconut milk. which is high in saturated fat. My revision is nearly indistinguishable from the original but all of the ingredients are readily available. it contains no saturated fat. and it is much lower in total calories. The soup must simmer for three or four hours. so I always do the first step in the recipe the day before. Making it ahead also improves the flavor.

> 8 cups defatted Chicken Stock (page 40)
> 1 teaspoon salt (omit if using salted stock)
> 6 garlic cloves, halved
> 1 bunch cilantro (fresh coriander), including roots if available, washed thoroughly
> Zest of 2 lemons
> 2 teaspoons crushed dried red pepper
> ¼ cup fresh lime juice
> 2 teaspoons coconut extract
> ½ pound elephant ear or oyster mushrooms
> 2 cups nonfat (skim) milk
> ½ cup chopped cilantro (fresh coriander), for garnish (optional)

1. In a saucepan. combine the stock. salt. garlic. cilantro. lemon peel. and red pepper and bring to a boil. Reduce heat as low as possible and simmer. uncovered. for 3 to 4 hours. (Do this the day ahead if you can.)

2. Strain the soup and return to the pan. Add the lime juice. coconut extract. and mushrooms and bring to a boil. Reduce the heat and simmer for 5 minutes. Add the milk. mix thoroughly. and remove from heat.

3. Ladle ¾ cup of soup into each of 8 cups. being careful to get approximately ¼ cup mushrooms with each serving. Top each serving of soup with 1 tablespoon chopped cilantro. (If reheating. do not allow to boil.)

MAKES EIGHT ¾-CUP SERVINGS

Each serving contains approximately:

Calories: 180	*Cholesterol: 1 mg*
Fat: 2 g	*Sodium: 258 mg*

CHINESE FIRECRACKER SALAD WITH THAI PEANUT DRESSING

This salad is designed to look like exploding fireworks, and it is just as exciting in taste as it is in appearance. If possible, make the dressing a day or two before you plan to use it so the flavors can blend. If you prefer less bite from the red pepper, reduce the amount by one-half.

You can also use the dressing as a sauce on Chuka Soba noodles—or any pasta for that matter—for a vegetarian entree.

DRESSING

> ⅓ cup rice wine vinegar
> ⅓ cup creamy unhomogenized peanut butter
> ¼ cup water
> 2 tablespoons sodium-reduced soy sauce
> 4 garlic cloves, quartered
> 1 tablespoon sugar
> 1 teaspoon crushed dried red pepper

SALAD

> 1 red bell pepper, seeded and membranes removed
> 1 yellow bell pepper, seeded and membranes removed
> 1 green bell pepper, seeded and membranes removed
> 8 green onions, white part only

1. Combine the dressing ingredients in a blender container and blend until smooth. Store tightly covered in the refrigerator. (Makes 1 cup or eight 2-tablespoon servings.)

2. Slice the peppers into very thin strips. Place the julienned peppers in a microwave-safe container and cover with plastic wrap. Microwave for 1 minute on high (or, if microwave is not available, steam peppers for 1 minute). Rinse peppers with cold water, drain thoroughly, and refrigerate until cold.

3. Cut the white ends of the green onions lengthwise into very thin strips and set aside.

4. Spoon 2 tablespoons of the dressing on each of 8 chilled plates. Arrange ¾ cup of the blanched peppers on top of the sauce, being careful to mix colors in order to resemble an exploding firecracker. Top each serving with strips of green onion.

MAKES 8 SERVINGS

Each serving contains approximately:

Calories: 87	*Cholesterol: 0 mg*
Fat: 6 g	*Sodium: 153 mg*

Chinese Firecracker Salad with Thai Peanut Dressing.

Seafood Potstickers.

SEAFOOD POTSTICKERS

❖

The most time-consuming part of making these potstickers is cleaning the spinach leaves. Although I always prefer the taste of fresh spinach over frozen. if your time is limited. use two 10-ounce packages of frozen chopped spinach. thawed and squeezed dry. These potstickers can also be made with poultry or meat. or—for a vegetarian dish—use tempeh. They make excellent hors d'oeuvres and can be served as a luncheon or dinner entree.

FILLING

1 pound fresh spinach leaves, stems and large veins removed, chopped; or 2 (10-ounce) packages frozen chopped spinach, thawed

1 egg white, lightly beaten

1 tablespoon sodium-reduced soy sauce

¼ teaspoon Chinese chili sauce

2 teaspoons peeled and minced fresh ginger

2 whole green onions, minced

½ pound cooked fish, flaked (2 cups)

SAUCE

½ cup water

1 tablespoon oyster sauce

½ teaspoon Chinese chili sauce

¼ teaspoon sugar

2 teaspoons grated orange zest

24 wonton skins
Cornstarch

2 tablespoons peanut oil

GARNISH

24 snow pea pods, strings removed and pods blanched

8 edible flowers, if available (pansies and nasturtiums)

1. Blanch the fresh spinach and drain thoroughly. being careful to squeeze out all moisture. If using frozen. simply squeeze out the moisture—it isn't necessary to cook it.

2. Combine the egg white. soy sauce. chili sauce. ginger, and green onions: mix thoroughly. Add the spinach and fish, and mix again.

3. In a separate bowl. combine the sauce ingredients and set aside.

4. Separate the wonton skins. Place 1 tablespoon of filling onto each of 24 wonton skins. Bring the 4 corners of each wonton skin into the center, overlapping to cover the filling and form a ball. Place the ball, folded side down, in the soft hollow of your hand between your thumb and index finger. Squeeze your hand together gently to form and seal each potsticker.

5. Place the finished potstickers on a large baking sheet that has been lightly dusted with cornstarch. Refrigerate uncovered. (Recipe to this point can be assembled several hours ahead and should be done at least 1 hour in advance.)

6. Heat the peanut oil in a large nonstick skillet over high heat. Add the potstickers and cook until bottoms are golden brown. Turn each potsticker to brown the other side. Pour sauce over potstickers, cover, and steam for 3 minutes. Remove cover and continue cooking until all the sauce is absorbed.

7. Cut a *V*-shaped notch at both ends of the pea pods and arrange 3 of them on each of 8 plates in a spoke pattern. Place 3 potstickers on each of the plates between the pea pods. Place a flower in the center of the plate.

MAKES 24 POTSTICKERS
Each potsticker contains approximately:

Calories: 70	Cholesterol: 13 mg
Fat: 2 g	Sodium: 51 mg

HOW TO FORM THE POTSTICKERS

1. Place one tablespoon of filling in the center of each wonton wrapper.

2. Fold one corner into the center.

3. Continue to fold, overlapping each corner.

4. Press to seal.

5. Place the potsticker fold-side down in the soft hollow of your hand between thumb and forefinger.

6. Squeeze your hand together gently to form a ball, holding it in place with the fingers of your other hand.

7. This process also seals the bottom of the potsticker "ball."

PORK TENDERLOIN IN TERIYAKI-PEAR SAUCE

◆

If you happen to have any of this pork left over, chop it up and mix it with the remaining sauce to serve over rice or noodles. In fact, I like it served this way so much that I sometimes make this pork just so I can do a noodle or rice dish for a buffet dinner.

> ¾ cup frozen unsweetened apple juice concentrate, undiluted
> ½ cup sodium-reduced soy sauce
> 2 garlic cloves, minced or pressed
> 1 tablespoon peeled and grated fresh ginger
> 2 pounds boneless pork tenderloin, all visible fat removed
> 1¼ pounds ripe pears, cored and peeled

1. If possible, at least one day before cooking the pork tenderloin, combine the apple juice concentrate, soy sauce, garlic, and ginger and mix well. Store, tightly covered, in the refrigerator.

2. Place the meat in a shallow, noncorrosive pan. Pour the marinade over the meat and cover tightly. Allow to stand in marinade at room temperature for 3 to 4 hours.

3. Preheat the oven to 350°F. Remove the meat from the marinade, reserving marinade for sauce. Place meat in a clean pan and roast uncovered for 30 minutes. Remove from oven and allow to stand for 10 to 15 minutes, then slice into ¼-inch-thick slices.

4. While the meat is roasting and resting, place the pears in a casserole and add enough water to fill ¼ inch from the bottom. Cover and bake pears in the oven with the pork for 30 to 40 minutes, or until soft. Pour marinade into a saucepan and bring to a boil. Boil rapidly for 3 minutes. Place baked pears in a food processor with a metal blade and puree (yields 1¼ cups). Add ¾ cup of the reduced marinade and blend well. Strain the sauce through a sieve or strainer to remove any lumps. Set aside.

5. To serve, place 6 or 7 slices on each plate. Spoon 2 tablespoons sauce over the top of each serving.

MAKES 8 SERVINGS
Each serving contains approximately:
Calories: 225   Cholesterol: 74 mg
Fat: 3 g   Sodium: 663 mg

CHUKA SOBA NOODLES

These curly noodles make a prettier presentation whether your meal is Oriental or not. Tossing them with the pungent dark sesame oil adds the flavor to complement the other foods on the plate. Chuka Soba noodles are available in Oriental markets.

> 6 cups water
> 8 ounces Chuka Soba noodles
> 1 tablespoon dark sesame oil

Bring the water to a boil. Add the noodles and cook for 2 to 3 minutes. Do not overcook! Stir to separate the noodles, then drain thoroughly and toss with sesame oil.

MAKES EIGHT ½-CUP SERVINGS
Each serving contains approximately:
Calories: 94   Cholesterol: 0 mg
Fat: 2 g   Sodium: 1 mg

STIR-FRIED SESAME ASPARAGUS

◆

The intense bright-green of this asparagus is perfect for adding color to the plate, while the sesame oil adds a sensational flavor. I sometimes make this and chill it to add to salads.

> *1¼ pounds fresh asparagus*
> *2 tablespoons dark sesame oil*

1. Cut off the tough ends of the asparagus and discard. Cut each spear diagonally into 1½-inch pieces.

2. Heat a skillet until a sprinkle of water dances in the pan. Add the sesame oil and tilt the pan to coat the bottom with the oil. Add the asparagus and stir-fry for about 2 to 3 minutes, or until it turns a very bright green.

MAKES EIGHT ½-CUP SERVINGS
Each serving contains approximately:

Calories: 53   *Cholesterol: 0 mg*
Fat: 4 g   *Sodium: 4 mg*

STICKY BLACK RICE PUDDING

◆

The first time I ever tasted this pudding was in a Thai restaurant in Dallas. I was so impressed with its unique taste and appearance that I asked for the recipe and immediately started working on a lighter version. The original recipe called for coconut milk, but I substituted coconut extract and added the mango puree, which I think enhances both the taste and the appearance of this unusual dessert. If fresh mangos are not available, use fresh papaya or peaches (fresh, frozen, or canned in juice).

> *1 cup sticky black (sweet) rice (available*
> *in Oriental markets)*
> *4 cups water*
> *¼ cup nonfat (skim) milk*
> *3 egg whites, lightly beaten*
> *3 tablespoons sugar*
> *1 tablespoon coconut extract*
> *1 8-ounce can water chestnuts, drained*
> *and diced (½ cup)*
> *1 8-ounce can crushed pineapple,*
> *thoroughly drained (⅔ cup)*
> *2 pounds mango, peeled, pitted,*
> *chopped, and pureed (2 cups)*
> *8 edible flowers for garnish, if available*

1. Bring the rice and water to a rapid boil. Continue to boil rapidly until all surface water has evaporated and top is covered with "craters." Reduce heat as low as possible and simmer, covered, for 20 minutes. Uncover and allow to cool to room temperature.

2. Combine the rice with the remaining ingredients except the mango and flowers, and mix well.

3. Preheat the oven to 325°F. Spoon the rice mixture into a casserole and bake uncovered for 45 minutes. Remove from oven and allow to come to room temperature. Refrigerate until cold.

4. Strain the mango puree and pour ¼ cup on each of 8 plates. Tilt each plate until puree covers the inner surface. Press some rice pudding into a ⅓-cup mold and then unmold onto the blade of a spatula. Place the molded rice pudding in the center of the puree and top each serving with a flower.

MAKES EIGHT ⅓-CUP SERVINGS
Each serving contains approximately:

Calories: 140   *Cholesterol: Negligible*
Fat: 1 g   *Sodium: 25 mg*

Formal Italian Dinner

❖

Marinated Eggplant Antipasto

Herbed Country Bread (page 81)

Risotto alla Milanese

Veal with Brandy Sauce

Tuscan Spinach with Raisins and Pine Nuts

Peaches in Champagne
with Biscotti d'Anise (page 82)

Italians can now claim the trendiest, most upscale restaurants in many cities throughout the world. Gone are the days when Italian restaurants were known by their checkered tablecloths, chianti bottles dripping with candle wax, and spaghetti topped with tomato sauce. This new wave of Italian haute cuisine is by no means "new" to Italy. It is simply the growing influence of Roman and Northern Italian cooking, which I have always admired for their elegance and subtlety.

I designed this formal dinner party menu with the help of a house guest from Rome, in whose honor I was giving the party. She prepared both the entree and the dessert, and I chronicled her every move, suggesting the use of lighter alternatives to her usual ingredients as we went along.

The eggplant appetizer, risotto, and Tuscan spinach are among my own favorite Italian dishes, and they balance the menu nicely, in both taste and texture. I serve the Herbed Country Bread with the appetizer because I think it goes so well with the pureed eggplant sauce.

Marinated Eggplant Antipasto

I use the smaller Japanese eggplant for this appetizer because the dish is prettier and better tasting that way; however, if they are not available, a larger eggplant certainly can be used. Just cut it into quarters or eighths lengthwise, depending on the size of the eggplants, to get the same general look on the plate.

I often make this as a spread or a dip rather than an appetizer. For a spread or dip, use eight eggplants rather than twelve. All other ingredients remain the same, however you do not need tomato or basil for a garnish.

> 12 *Japanese eggplants (3 pounds)*
> ¼ *cup balsamic vinegar*
> ¼ *cup extra-virgin olive oil*
> 2 *tablespoons chopped fresh parsley*
> 2 *garlic cloves*
> 1 *teaspoon fresh thyme, or ½ teaspoon dried, crushed*
> 1 *teaspoon salt*
> ¼ *teaspoon freshly ground black pepper*
> ¼ *teaspoon dried red pepper flakes*
> 8 *plum tomatoes, peeled and quartered*
> 8 *sprigs basil, for garnish (optional)*

1. Steam or microwave the eggplants until they can easily be pierced with a fork, about 3 to 5 minutes. Peel the eggplants and place in a bowl. Pour the vinegar over the eggplants and allow to cool completely, turning frequently to completely marinate.

2. Slice 4 eggplants in half lengthwise and set aside. Chop the remaining 8 eggplants and place in a food processor. Add the vinegar marinade, olive oil, parsley, garlic, thyme, salt, pepper and red pepper. Blend until smooth (makes 2⅔ cups). Set aside.

3. Arrange an eggplant half on each of 8 plates. Place ⅓ cup of the eggplant sauce on the side. Garnish plates with 4 tomato quarters and a sprig of basil. Serve with Herbed Country Bread (page 81).

MAKES 8 SERVINGS WITHOUT BREAD
Each serving contains approximately:
Calories: 113   *Cholesterol: 0 mg*
Fat: 7 g   *Sodium: 305 mg*

Risotto alla Milanese

The two ingredients necessary for a perfect risotto are Arborio rice and plenty of patience. Arborio rice is a small, white opaque grain unique to the north of Italy. Risotto is made by cooking this rice slowly, adding the stock a little at a time, and stirring constantly until a creamy, cereal-like consistency is achieved. It simply cannot be rushed!

Risotto alla Milanese is classically seasoned with saffron, which adds a wonderful color as well as a sensational taste. I often serve risotto as a second course for an Italian dinner instead of a pasta because it is more unusual.

> 3 *tablespoons corn oil margarine*
> 1 *medium onion, finely chopped (1½ cups)*
> 1¼ *cups Arborio rice*
> 1 *cup dry white wine*
> ½ *teaspoon saffron threads*
> 6 *cups defatted Chicken Stock (page 40), boiling*
> ¾ *teaspoon salt (omit if using salted stock)*
> ½ *teaspoon freshly ground black pepper*
> 8 *ounces freshly grated Parmesan cheese (2 cups)*
> 8 *sprigs Italian parsley, for garnish*

1. Melt the margarine in a large heavy pot over medium heat. Add the onion and cook stirring frequently until soft and translucent, about 10 minutes. Add the rice and stir until each grain is coated and shiny. Add the wine and cook until almost dry. Dissolve the saffron in a little of the boiling stock, and then add the stock to the rice mixture. Continue to add the stock ½ cup at a time, stirring constantly until each addition is almost absorbed. (There should always be a "veil" of stock over the rice.)

2. When the rice is the consistency of creamy porridge and the grains are soft, in about 20 minutes, remove from heat and add the salt, pepper, and 1½ cups of the cheese, reserving ½ cup for garnish. Mix well.

3. Spoon ¾ cup risotto onto each of 8 plates or into shallow bowls. Top each serving with 1 tablespoon of grated Parmesan and a sprig of parsley.

MAKES EIGHT ¾-CUP SERVINGS
Each serving contains approximately:
Calories: 287   *Cholesterol: 15 mg*
Fat: 11 g   *Sodium: 682 mg*

Marinated Eggplant Antipasto.

Risotto alla Milanese.

VEAL WITH BRANDY SAUCE

This fabulous-tasting veal, the creation of my Italian house-guest, was changed only slightly from her original recipe. I encouraged her to use low-fat milk instead of cream, and she told us that she honestly could not tell the difference in the finished dish. All of the guests cried "Bravo!"

  2 tablespoons corn oil margarine
  2 medium onions, finely chopped
    (3 cups)
  2 pounds boneless veal tenderloin (see
    Note)
  ½ cup cognac or brandy
  24 fresh mushroom caps, cleaned and
    stems cut off
  1 cup 2% low-fat milk, warmed
  ¼ teaspoon salt
  ⅛ teaspoon freshly ground black pepper

1. Preheat the oven to 350°F. Melt the margarine in a heavy skillet, then add the onions and cook until soft, about 10 minutes. Add the veal and sauté until well browned on all sides. Remove veal from pan and place in a dry baking dish. Bake for 10 minutes or until desired degree of doneness. Remove veal from oven and allow to stand for 5 minutes before slicing.

2. Deglaze the pan with brandy. Add the mushroom caps, milk, salt, and pepper. Mix well and simmer, covered, for 10 minutes.

3. Remove mushroom caps and set aside. Pour milk mixture into a blender container and blend until smooth.

4. Slice the veal tenderloin into 24 slices. Arrange 3 slices on each of 8 plates. Top each slice with a mushroom cap. Pour 1 tablespoon of the sauce over the top of each mushroom and serve.

MAKES 8 SERVINGS
Each serving contains approximately:
  Calories: 269   Cholesterol: 87 mg
  Fat: 15 g   Sodium: 186 mg

N O T E : Beef tenderloin may be substituted for the veal in this recipe but the nutritional information is for veal.

TUSCAN SPINACH WITH RAISINS AND PINE NUTS

This is a dish totally dependent on using fresh spinach. It is also important to remove the large stems and veins from each leaf, since they are bitter tasting and tough.

  1 cup raisins
  ¼ cup pine nuts
  6 pounds fresh spinach
  2 tablespoons extra-virgin olive oil
  ½ teaspoon salt

1. Soak the raisins in warm water for about 30 minutes: drain and pat dry. While raisins are soaking, preheat the oven to 350°F. Toast the pine nuts for about 3 minutes or until golden brown. Watch carefully, as they burn easily. Set aside.

2. Remove the stems and large veins from the spinach and steam it for 1½ minutes. Rinse the spinach under cold running water to set the color: drain thoroughly.

3. Heat the olive oil and salt in a large skillet. Sauté the spinach and raisins in the hot oil until the spinach is thoroughly heated. (You may have to do this in two batches.) Top each serving with 1½ teaspoons of the toasted pine nuts.

MAKES EIGHT ½-CUP SERVINGS
Each serving contains approximately:
  Calories: 186   Cholesterol: 0 mg
  Fat: 7 g   Sodium: 419 mg

Tuscan Spinach with Raisins and Pine Nuts.

PEACHES IN CHAMPAGNE

When fresh peaches are not available for Peaches in Champagne you can use fresh pears, which are available all year round.

2 pounds fresh peaches
¼ cup fresh lemon juice
1 tablespoon sugar
1 split (small bottle) champagne

1. Peel the peaches, cut in half, and remove pits. Cut in half-inch long, finger-size slices (4 cups).

2. Put the sliced peaches in a bowl, add the lemon juice and sugar, and mix well. Pour the champagne over the peaches, cover tightly, and allow to marinate in the refrigerator for several hours before serving.

MAKES EIGHT ½-CUP SERVINGS
(WITH MARINADE)

Each serving contains approximately:

Calories: 74   *Cholesterol: 0 mg*
Fat: Negligible   *Sodium: 2 mg*

Peaches in Champagne and Amaretto di Saronno are a fitting finale to this Italian meal.

A Few of My Favorite Things

❖

Perfect Red Pepper Soup

Sautéed Snails with Walnuts

Gingered Pepper Salmon with Cabernet Sauce

Lemon Linguine with Salmon Caviar

Vegetable Bouquet

Cinnamon-Apple Wonder

Here is a wonderfully eclectic and many-faceted menu. As the title suggests, it is composed of some of my all-time favorites. Three of these recipes were "gifts" from very talented chefs, who shared them with me so I could lighten their original recipes. I think they are among the best and most unusual dishes I've ever tasted.

Among my favorite decorating ideas is putting a lace tablecloth over a solid colored one and then matching the napkins to the color of the cloth.

Sautéed Snails with Walnuts

This is a variation of Philippe Van Cappellen's original recipe —he uses almonds, a bit more oil, and real sour cream. I prefer the taste of walnuts with Belgian endive, so I use walnut oil instead of olive oil to sauté the snails and reinforce the flavor of the nuts. This dish can also be served as an appetizer.

½ cup coarsely chopped walnuts
24 canned snails (200-gram can), drained, rinsed, and dried
2 tablespoons walnut oil
⅛ teaspoon salt
⅛ teaspoon freshly ground black pepper
2 teaspoons Dijon mustard
¼ cup balsamic vinegar
¼ cup water
½ cup light sour cream
8 to 10 Belgian endive, julienned (6 cups), reserving 24 outer leaves for garnish

1. Place the walnuts in a 350°F. oven for 8 to 10 minutes, or until golden brown. Watch carefully—they burn easily! Set aside.

2. Rinse and dry snails. Heat the walnut oil in a sauté pan and sauté the snails until browned, about 5 minutes. Remove snails from pan and set aside. Add the salt, pepper, mustard, vinegar, and water to the pan; mix thoroughly and bring to a boil. Remove from heat and add the sour cream, mixing thoroughly.

3. Place ¾ cup julienned endive on each of 8 plates to form a circular bed. Place 3 whole endive leaves on top of the bed, radiating out like the spokes of a wheel and dividing the plates into thirds. Place 3 snails in the center of each plate and spoon 2 tablespoons of sauce over the top. Sprinkle 1 tablespoon walnuts over the top of each serving.

MAKES 8 SERVINGS
Each serving contains approximately:
Calories: 130   Cholesterol: 18 mg
Fat: 10 g   Sodium: 86 mg

With the Gingered Pepper Salmon, I serve the same Cabernet I use to make the sauce.

Gingered Pepper Salmon with Cabernet Sauce

The River Café in Brooklyn is one of my favorite restaurants in the world, for both the ambiance and the food. The first time I ever tasted this salmon dish I was sitting by the window looking across the river at the Manhattan skyline. The River Café's imaginative and superb chef, David Burke, calls this dish Gingered Salmon in Burgundy Butter. It was easily the most delicious salmon I had ever tasted so I asked David for the recipe and immediately went to work on revising it. Since I couldn't use butter, I also had to revise the name. I'm happy to report that David was as pleased with my revision as I was.

The first time I served this dish for a dinner party, I ordered a fresh salmon flown in from Seattle. When the enormous salmon arrived packed in ice, I had to have help just carrying it to the kitchen. The lengthy process of filleting the whole fish is unnecessary for this recipe, so I recommend that you order salmon fillets from your local fish market.

> 8 ounces fresh ginger, peeled and diced
> 1 bottle Cabernet Sauvignon or other dry red wine (about 4 cups)
> 6 shallots, minced (⅔ cup)
> 3 tablespoons corn oil margarine
> ¼ teaspoon salt
> 2 pounds fresh salmon fillet, center cut across the grain
> 2 tablespoons cracked black peppercorns
> 2 tablespoons extra-virgin olive oil

1. Put the diced ginger in a saucepan and cover with water. Bring to a boil and simmer for 15 minutes. Drain and repeat 2 times. Drain thoroughly, then puree the ginger in a food processor until smooth and pastelike (¾ cup); set aside.

2. Combine the wine and shallots in a heavy saucepan and bring to a boil. Simmer until only 1 cup wine remains. Add the margarine a little at a time, stirring constantly. Add the salt, mix well, and cover to keep warm.

3. Remove the skin from the salmon and also, with tweezers, any little vertical bones. Cut into 8 equal portions, then spread a thin layer (1½ tablespoons) of the ginger puree on top of each portion and sprinkle evenly with cracked peppercorns.

4. Heat the oil in a skillet large enough for all 8 portions of salmon. When the skillet is very hot, sauté the salmon, ginger side down, for 2 minutes. Turn the fish and sear other side just to seal; do not overcook. Remove the fish from pan and place on paper towel ginger side up.

5. Spoon 2 tablespoons of the sauce on each of 8 plates and top with the salmon.

MAKES 8 SERVINGS

Each serving contains approximately:
Calories: 264   Cholesterol: 42 mg
Fat: 14 g   Sodium: 187 mg

Lemon Linguine with Salmon Caviar

The flavor and texture of the linguine are nice accompaniments for the very spicy salmon, as is the Vegetable Bouquet that follows. Lemon Linguine also makes a tasty pasta entree combined with chicken or any seafood.

> 1 tablespoon lemon zest
> 2 tablespoons fresh lemon juice
> 1 tablespoon extra-virgin olive oil
> ¼ teaspoon salt
> 1 garlic clove, pressed or minced (1 teaspoon)
> 1 pound linguine
> 8 teaspoons salmon caviar (1 2-ounce jar)

1. Combine all ingredients except the linguine and caviar, and mix well. Set aside.

2. Cook the linguine in 4 quarts of boiling water for 5 to 6 minutes or until al dente (slightly resistant to the bite). Drain thoroughly. Place the pasta in a large bowl and add the lemon-oil mixture. Mix thoroughly.

3. Place ½ cup linguine on each of 8 plates and twist into ball-like shapes. Top each ball with 1 teaspoon salmon caviar.

MAKES 8 SERVINGS

Each ½ cup contains approximately:
Calories: 106   Cholesterol: 27 mg
Fat: 2 g   Sodium: 81 mg

VEGETABLE BOUQUET

❖

16 asparagus spears
2 yellow summer squash, thinly sliced
   into 24 rounds
2 zucchini, thinly sliced into 24 rounds
4 carrots, peeled and cut into 32
   "flowers" (as illustrated on page 107)

Steam the vegetables separately until crisp-tender. Arrange the vegetables—2 asparagus spears, 3 yellow squash slices, 3 zucchini slices, and 4 carrot "flowers"—decoratively on each plate.

MAKES 8 SERVINGS

Each serving contains approximately:

Calories: 40   Cholesterol: 0 mg
Fat: Negligible   Sodium: 11 mg

HOW TO CREATE CARROT FLOWERS

❖

1. Using a sharp paring knife, make four diagonal cuts of equal size into the large end of the peeled carrot.

2. After the fourth cut, just snap the "flower" off of the carrot.

3. Continue until you have the desired number of carrot flowers. Another use for steamed carrot flowers is as candle holders on carrot birthday cakes.

CINNAMON-APPLE WONDER

The inspiration for this dessert was called "The Ultimate Apple Killer" at the Forge Restaurant in Miami Beach, and it was created by Chef Kal Abdalla.

> 2 tablespoons corn oil margarine
> ½ cup packed dark brown sugar
> ¼ cup ground cinnamon
> 2 pounds golden Delicious apples, peeled, cored, and thinly sliced
> 1 tablespoon vanilla extract
> ¼ cup fresh lemon juice
> 18 phyllo dough leaves, at room temperature
> Confectioners' sugar, for garnish
> Nonstick vegetable spray

1. Melt the margarine in a large pan. Add the brown sugar and cinnamon and mix well. Add the apples and cook until they start to soften. Add the vanilla and lemon juice, and cook until apples are soft. The cooking time should not exceed 10 minutes. Cool.

2. Place one leaf of phyllo dough on a flat surface and coat with nonstick vegetable spray. Place a second leaf on top and spray again. Repeat with a third leaf, then cut the leaves crosswise.

3. Coat the inside of a custard cup or ½-cup ramekin with nonstick spray and place the end of one of the strips of phyllo in the bottom of the dish, shaping it to the inside of the dish and leaving the other end extending over the edge and onto the work surface. Repeat with remaining strips, overlapping, clockwise, in a circle around the edge of the dish with the inner ends stacked on the bottom of the dish.

4. Fill the phyllo cup with ½ cup of the apple mixture and pull the strips together, overlapping one strip at a time to form a "purse." When they have been gathered together at the top, close them with a light twist and then separate the leaves above the twist for a fanned effect.

5. Preheat the oven to 325°F. and then bake for 15 minutes or until lightly browned. To serve, place each dessert on a plate and dust with a sprinkling of sugar.

MAKES 6 SERVINGS

Each serving contains approximately:
Calories: 346   Cholesterol: 0 mg
Fat: 4 g   Sodium: 285 mg

HOW TO FORM CINNAMON-APPLE WONDER

1. Coat one sheet of phyllo with non-stick vegetable spray.

2. Repeat the process with the second and third sheets.

3. Cut the sheets into 6 equal strips.

4. Place one end of the strip in the bottom of custard cup or ramekin that has been coated with nonstick vegetable spray.

5. Repeat with remaining 5 strips overlapping in circle so that the ends are stacked in the bottom of the cup.

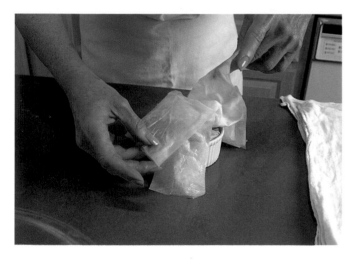

8. Separate the leaves about the twist.

9. Now arrange the leaves to form a fanned effect. Bake.

6. After filling the cup with ½ cup of the apple mixture, start bringing the strips together, overlapping each one.

7. When you've gathered all the strips, close them with a light twist.

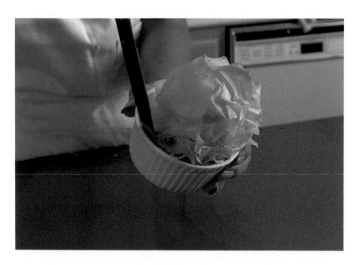

10. Let cool until you can handle the cup. Loosen around the edge with a metal spatula or knife and then unmold.

11. Place each Cinnamon-Apple Wonder in the center of a dinner-sized plate, and sprinkle lightly with powdered sugar.

Black and White After-the-Theater Champagne Supper

❖

Vichyssoise with Caviar

Black Linguine with White Clam Sauce

Belgian Endive Salad with Goat Cheese Dressing and Black Walnuts

White Port–Poached Pears on Chocolate Sauce

In most places there are so few restaurants open for after-theater dining that a small party at home offers a festive and fun alternative. It allows both the hosts and guests to critique the entertainment of the evening in an intimate and gracious setting.

After-the-theater entertaining differs from other types of dinner parties in that the hour is late, your guests have probably had pretheater cocktails, and they do not feel like waiting before being served. I have designed this supper menu to include only foods that go well with champagne and which require no more than ten minutes to prepare from the time you arrive home from the theater to the actual serving of the supper. The black and white theme of the meal matches my decor as well as adds a dramatic and whimsical touch to the party.

VICHYSSOISE WITH CAVIAR

This vichyssoise is the most delicious and easy-to-make version of the classic soup I have come up with to date. The touches of lemon and sour cream also go extremely well with the caviar. Vichyssoise should be served very cold, in either chilled bowls or icers. And it should be made early in the day or the day before and stored, covered, in the refrigerator.

> 2 medium baking potatoes (1 pound),
>   peeled and diced
> 1 large white onion, chopped (2 cups)
> 1½ cups defatted Chicken Stock
>   (page 40)
> ½ cup nonfat (skim) milk
> ½ cup light sour cream
> ½ teaspoon salt (omit if using salted
>   stock)
> 2 teaspoons fresh lemon juice
> ½ cup minced onion
> ¼ cup caviar

1. Combine the diced potatoes and chopped onion in a large saucepan. Add the chicken stock and bring to a boil. Reduce the heat and simmer, covered, until the potatoes are soft, about 20 minutes.

2. Spoon the cooked potato mixture into a blender container or food processor and add all remaining ingredients except the minced onion and caviar. Blend until smooth, then refrigerate, covered, until cold.

3. Pour ½ cup of cold soup into each of 8 chilled bowls. Top each serving with 1 tablespoon minced onion and ½ tablespoon caviar.

MAKES EIGHT ½-CUP SERVINGS

Each serving contains approximately:

Calories: 100   Cholesterol: 54 mg
Fat: 4 g   Sodium: 300 mg

BLACK LINGUINE WITH WHITE CLAM SAUCE

This pasta is as tasty as it is terrific looking. This is perhaps my favorite pasta dish for any occasion and is certainly perfect for this menu. It is the only course that you prepare at the time of the party, and, if you have everything premeasured and ready to put together ahead of time, it only takes a few minutes.

> 4   (6½-ounce) cans chopped clams, with
>   juice
> ½   teaspoon salt
> ¼   teaspoon freshly ground black pepper
> ¼   cup dry sherry
> 2   teaspoons grated lemon peel
> 2   tablespoons cornstarch
> 1½ cups (1 12-ounce can) evaporated
>   skim milk
> ½   cup freshly grated Parmesan cheese
> 1   tablespoon fresh lemon juice
> 2   pounds fresh black (squid ink)
>   linguine noodles
> 1   tablespoon extra-virgin olive oil
> 8   clams in the shell, scrubbed and
>   steamed until open
> 8   lemon peel strips, for ties

1. Drain the liquid from the clams into a saucepan. Set drained clams aside. Add the salt, pepper, sherry, and lemon peel, then bring the mixture to a boil and reduce heat to a simmer.

2. Combine the cornstarch and evaporated milk and stir until cornstarch is dissolved. Slowly add to the simmering liquid, stirring constantly with a wire whisk. Continue to stir until slightly thickened. Remove from the heat, then add cheese, lemon juice, and clams. Mix well and cover to keep warm.

3. Cook the pasta until al dente, about 2 to 3 minutes. Drain thoroughly and toss with olive oil. Place 1 cup of cooked pasta on each of 8 heated plates. Top each serving with ½ cup sauce and garnish with a steamed clam and a peel of lemon tied in a knot.

MAKES 8 SERVINGS
Each serving contains approximately:

Calories: 310   Cholesterol: 44 mg

Fat: 5 g   Sodium: 832 mg

BELGIAN ENDIVE SALAD WITH GOAT CHEESE DRESSING AND BLACK WALNUTS

The salad is the perfect change of pace in both taste and texture to follow the soup and pasta. The dressing should be made the day before. The salads can be plated, covered with plastic wrap, and refrigerated. The walnuts are already toasted and ready to go on the salad before you leave for the theater. All you have to do before serving is unwrap each salad and top it with the dressing and walnuts.

> ½ cup black walnut pieces
> 10 small heads Belgian endive
>   (1¼ pounds)
> 1 cup Goat Cheese Dressing (page 120)

1. Place the walnuts in a 350°F. oven for 8 to 10 minutes or until golden brown. Watch carefully, as they burn easily. Set aside.

2. Julienne 8 of the endive heads (you should have 6 cups). Separate the remaining 2 heads into leaves for a garnish.

3. Place ¾ cup of julienned endive onto each of 8 chilled plates. Top each salad with 2 tablespoons dressing. Garnish with the reserved endive leaves and top each with 1 tablespoon toasted black walnuts.

MAKES 8 SERVINGS
Each serving contains approximately:
Calories: 78   Cholesterol: 2 mg
Fat: 6 g   Sodium: 133 mg

WHITE PORT–POACHED PEARS ON CHOCOLATE SAUCE

This dessert is a delightful finishing touch to the menu because it is so elegant in appearance. Both the sauce and the pears should be made the day before the party.

> 8 ripe pears with stems
> 4 cinnamon sticks
> 1 magnum (1.5 liters) white port wine
>   (a domestic or other inexpensive port)
> 1½ cups Chocolate Sauce (page 57)

1. Using an apple corer, remove the core from the blossom end of each pear, being careful not to disturb the stem. Using a potato peeler, peel each pear, leaving the peeled surface as smooth as possible. Place the cored, peeled pears in a deep saucepan large enough to hold all of the pears well below the top of the pan. Add cinnamon sticks. Pour enough wine over the pears to completely cover them.

2. Bring the wine to a boil, reduce the heat, and simmer, uncovered, for 5 to 10 minutes or until pears can easily be pierced with a fork. Remove the saucepan from heat and allow to cool to room temperature.

3. Cover the saucepan and refrigerate for 24 hours to give the pears time to absorb the flavor of the wine.

4. To serve, spoon 3 tablespoons of the chocolate sauce into the bottom of each of 8 shallow bowls. Remove the pears from the wine and place each one, stem up, on top of the sauce. (Reserve poaching liquid for a hot or cold nonalcoholic beverage —the cooling process removes the alcohol from the port.)

MAKES 8 SERVINGS
Each serving contains approximately:
Calories: 225   Cholesterol: 1 mg
Fat: 3 g   Sodium: 66 mg

Candlelight Dinner for Two

❖

*Salad of Young Greens with
Goat Cheese Dressing*

Whole Wheat–Thyme Rolls (page 43)

*Breast of Chicken in Rosemary "Cream" Sauce
with Root Vegetables, Leeks, and Mushrooms*

Cold Lemon Soufflé

Set the scene for a romantic evening at home alone with that special someone in your life. This is a perfect menu for an occasion such as an anniversary or a birthday. Or make any occasion "special" with this intimate dinner for two.

I chose a small table in the living room near the fireplace to set the scene for this party. Since I don't have table pads for this size table, I use wooden service plates and leave them on the table for the entree rather than removing them with the first course.

I also use candles large enough to provide adequate light for the room. Having just candlelight is not only romantic, it is very flattering. Individually calligraphed menus always add a special aura to a meal, but when it's just dinner for two, your guest will feel even more special. The menu is designed to be prepared in advance so that you don't have to spend much time in the kitchen the evening of your party.

SALAD OF YOUNG GREENS WITH GOAT CHEESE DRESSING

❖

This salad can be plated, wrapped with plastic wrap, and refrigerated hours ahead of time. The dressing should be made the day before to ensure the flavors blend properly.

> 2 cups assorted young greens (Belgian
>   endive, radicchio, watercress, Bibb
>   lettuce, arugula, and so on)
> ¼ cup Goat Cheese Dressing (recipe
>   follows)

Arrange the greens on 2 chilled plates. Top each serving with 2 tablespoons dressing.

MAKES 2 SERVINGS

Each serving contains approximately:
*Calories: 31   Cholesterol: 2 mg
Fat: 2 g   Sodium: 132 mg*

1. Combine all the ingredients except the cottage cheese in a blender or food processor with a metal blade and blend until smooth. Pour into a bowl and add cottage cheese. Mix well.

2. Store, tightly covered, in the refrigerator.

MAKES 2 CUPS; SIXTEEN 2-TABLESPOON SERVINGS

Each serving contains approximately:

Calories: 33	*Cholesterol: 5 mg*
Fat: 1 g	*Sodium: 164 mg*

Salad of Young Greens with Goat Cheese Dressing.

GOAT CHEESE DRESSING

❖

1 cup buttermilk

½ cup silken soft tofu

3 ounces goat cheese (about ⅓ cup, packed)

1½ teaspoons canola or corn oil

1½ teaspoons freshly squeezed lemon juice

1 garlic clove, quartered

½ teaspoon salt

¼ teaspoon freshly ground black pepper

¼ cup low-fat cottage cheese

BREAST OF CHICKEN IN ROSEMARY "CREAM" SAUCE WITH ROOT VEGETABLES, LEEKS, AND MUSHROOMS

❖

The reason for reducing the stock here is to intensify the flavor; if you are using a flavorful stock, this step is less necessary. Don't worry if your sauce breaks down and looks rather dreadful before the cooking time is over. Blending it will smooth it out again, and straining it gives it a satin-smooth texture. This is the only course that requires preparation the evening of your dinner. If you have all your ingredients prepared ahead of time, it will require very little time away from your guest.

3 leeks, roots removed

1 tablespoon canola or corn oil

¼ pound fresh mushrooms, sliced

2 cups defatted Chicken Stock (page 40)

1 onion, finely chopped (1½ cups)

½ cup dry white wine

½ cup canned evaporated skim milk

1 whole chicken breast (8 ounces), boned and skinned

¼ teaspoon fresh rosemary leaves, or pinch of dried

⅛ teaspoon salt (omit if using salted stock)

Dash of freshly ground black pepper

¼ teaspoon fresh lemon juice

12 baby carrots, steamed

6 new red potatoes, steamed

2 rosemary sprigs, or garnish (optional)

1. Trim one of the leeks to about 6 inches in length, including at least 1 inch of the green end. Starting at the white end of the leek, halve the leek lengthwise, then repeat with each half to make four 6-inch-long pieces of leek. Separate the strips of leek and steam or microwave the strips until soft; set aside.

2. Chop only the white parts of the remaining 2 leeks. Heat the oil over low heat in a heavy pan. Add the chopped leeks and cook, covered, until soft, about 10 minutes. Add the mushrooms and continue to cook, covered, until the mushrooms are soft (about 5 minutes). Remove from heat; keep covered.

3. Bring the stock to a boil and reduce by half. Combine the chopped onion and wine in a saucepan and cook until dry. Add the 1 cup of reduced stock and the evaporated milk and simmer, uncovered, until almost dry, about 25 minutes.

4. Preheat the oven to 350°F. Place the chicken breast in a baking dish and bake, covered, for 15 minutes. Remove from the oven and leave covered for at least 10 minutes more. Cut the breast in half, removing and discarding center cartilage. Butterfly each half-breast.

5. Pour the stock mixture into a blender container. Add the rosemary, salt, pepper, and lemon juice and blend until smooth. Pour the sauce through a sieve.

6. Arrange the steamed leek strips in a basket pattern in the center of 2 plates. Spoon ½ cup of the leek-mushroom mixture on each basket. Top with a butterflied chicken breast, wrapping over and around to conceal the leek mixture. Pour half the sauce over each chicken breast. Arrange 6 carrots and 3 potatoes around the rim of each plate. Garnish each serving with a sprig of rosemary, if desired.

MAKES 2 SERVINGS
Each serving contains approximately:
Calories: 425   *Cholesterol: 75 mg*
Fat: 12 g   *Sodium: 397 mg*

COLD LEMON SOUFFLÉ

This dramatic and delicious soufflé is sure to impress even the most discriminating diner. Its light texture and delicate flavor are further enhanced by the raspberry sauce. I call it "Secret" sauce because it tastes so complex and it is so easy to make. Never tell anyone how you made it!

    2 envelopes unflavored gelatin
    ½ cup water
    1 egg yolk
    1 12-ounce can frozen lemonade
       concentrate, undiluted and thawed
       (1½ cups)
    6 egg whites
    ¾ cup canned evaporated skim milk,
       well chilled
    1 teaspoon finely grated lemon peel
       Lemon zest, for garnish (optional)
       Raspberry Sauce (recipe follows)

1. Wrap a 5- or 6-inch soufflé dish with a wax paper collar standing at least 4 inches above the top. Tape it in place with masking tape. (See illustration.) Set aside.

2. Soften the gelatin in the water for 5 minutes. Beat the egg yolk with a wire whisk until creamy, then combine the gelatin and egg yolk in the top of a double boiler and place over simmering water. Heat, stirring constantly, until the gelatin has completely dissolved. This does not take long, so make sure to stir constantly until you can no longer see gelatin on a metal spoon. Do not boil!

3. Remove from the heat and add the lemonade concentrate. Mix well and pour into a large bowl. Refrigerate until syrupy, about 30 minutes.

4. Beat the egg whites until stiff but not dry. Set aside, wash beaters well, then rinse with cold water so they are no longer warm to the touch. Beat the evaporated milk until it has increased about 4 times in volume and soft peaks form.

5. Fold the beaten milk, gently but thoroughly, into the cold lemon mixture using a rubber spatula. Fold the egg whites in until no streaks of white show. Carefully pour the soufflé mixture into the prepared soufflé dish. Refrigerate for at least 4 hours, then remove the collar to serve.

6. Sprinkle the top of the soufflé with lemon zest for garnish. Slice into wedges and spoon ¼ cup of sauce over the top of each serving.

N O T E : This recipe makes 12 servings of soufflé, while I have included only 2 servings of sauce. I always make the entire soufflé recipe. The presentation is so much more dramatic and leftovers freeze beautifully for a tasty and light frozen dessert. Do not make more sauce than you intend to serve. To make enough sauce for the entire soufflé, multiply the recipe by 6.

M A K E S   1 2   ⅔ - C U P   S E R V I N G S
Each serving (with sauce) contains approximately:
Calories: 155   Cholesterol: 23 mg
Fat: 2 g   Sodium: 74 mg

RASPBERRY SAUCE

    ½ cup melted vanilla ice milk
    2 tablespoons fresh or frozen raspberries
    1 teaspoon Grand Marnier

Combine the ingredients in a blender container and blend until smooth. Pour through a sieve to remove raspberry seeds.

M A K E S   ½   C U P ;   T W O   ¼ - C U P   S E R V I N G S
Each serving contains approximately:
Calories: 60   Cholesterol: 5 mg
Fat: 1 g   Sodium: 27 mg

Culberton's Train Champagne is the official champagne of the
American-European Express.

A Trip on the Orient Express

❖

*Hearts of Palm Salad
with Papaya Vinaigrette*

*Curried Breast of Pheasant under Glass
with Gingered Fruit Pilaf and
Toasted Pine Nuts*

Frozen Lemon Cloud

The next time you invite a friend over to watch a video, why not match the menu to the theme of the movie? For example, you could serve the Formal Italian Dinner while watching *Roman Holiday* or use the New Year's Day Southern Style menu for *Gone with the Wind, Glass Menagerie,* or *Cat on a Hot Tin Roof.* The Best of the Southwest menu pairs well with almost any western.

For *Murder on the Orient Express,* I decided to emulate a dinner served on the famous train itself. I ordered the china, crystal, silver, and accessories used in the dining car and served Culbertson's Train Cuvee, which is the official champagne of the new American-European Express that runs between Chicago and Washington, D.C. The menu, too, was designed to be as similar as possible to the cuisine of that great, elegant train.

The menu here is for two persons, but it is easily expanded for several more people without taking much more time. I have limited it to three courses so that you don't have to stop the movie more than twice after you start watching it.

HEARTS OF PALM SALAD WITH PAPAYA VINAIGRETTE

❖

A salad that is as easy to prepare as salad gets! It is spectacular for large groups and goes well with a wide variety of other menu items.

> ½ cup Papaya Vinaigrette (recipe
> follows)
> 4 hearts of palm, cut on the diagonal
> into ½-inch pieces
> Italian parsley, for garnish (optional)

Spoon ¼ cup of vinaigrette on the bottoms of 2 plates. Arrange the hearts of palm pieces on top. Garnish with parsley.

MAKES 2 SERVINGS
Each serving contains approximately:
Calories: 75   Cholesterol: 0 mg
Fat: 2 g   Sodium: 6 mg

Hearts of Palm Salad with Papaya Vinaigrette.

PAPAYA VINAIGRETTE

½ small papaya (½ pound), peeled and
   diced
1½ teaspoons fresh lime juice
1½ teaspoons raspberry vinegar
¾ teaspoon unsweetened frozen
   pineapple juice concentrate,
   undiluted
½ teaspoon canola or corn oil
   Dash of cayenne pepper

Combine all ingredients in a blender container and blend until
smooth. Pour through a sieve to strain.

MAKES ½ CUP; TWO ¼-CUP SERVINGS
Each serving contains approximately:
   Calories: 45   *Cholesterol: 0 mg*
   Fat: 1 g   *Sodium: 2 mg*

CURRIED BREAST OF PHEASANT UNDER GLASS WITH GINGERED FRUIT PILAF AND TOASTED PINE NUTS

This is a rather long recipe but not difficult, and the preparation
works well for a variety of other dishes. Chicken breast can be
substituted for the pheasant. You could substitute an herbed
pilaf and the Rosemary "Cream" Sauce on page 122. If you don't
have time to make the chutney called for in the sauce, substitute
a prepared chutney.

  2 tablespoons pine nuts
  1 whole pheasant breast
  1 cup Gingered Fruit Pilaf (recipe follows)
  1 medium onion, chopped (1½ cups)
  ½ cup dry white wine
1½ cups defatted Chicken Stock (page 40)
  ¾ teaspoon curry powder
  ⅛ teaspoon salt (omit if using salted stock)
  ½ teaspoon fresh lemon juice
  1 tablespoon Pear Chutney (page 130)

1. Preheat the oven to 350°F. Place the pine nuts in a pan and
bake for about 3 minutes or until golden brown. Watch carefully,
as they burn easily. Set aside.

2. Bone the pheasant breast, leaving wings intact. (See illustra-
tion.) Remove skin from breast but leave skin on wing bones.
Cut breast in half. Remove center cartilage and all visible fat.
Place ½ cup of the pilaf in the center of each pheasant breast.
Fold the bottom half of the breast over the pilaf and roll tightly,
securing with wing bone.

3. Place breasts in a baking dish that has been coated with
nonstick vegetable spray and bake, covered, for 20 minutes.
Remove from oven and leave covered for 10 more minutes.

4. Combine the chopped onion and wine in a heavy saucepan
and bring to a boil. Reduce the heat and cook, uncovered, until
dry. Add the stock and curry powder; simmer, stirring frequently,
until greatly reduced in volume, about 25 minutes. Spoon the
mixture into a blender container. Add salt and lemon juice and
blend until smooth. Press sauce through a sieve, then stir in the
chutney.

5. Transfer pheasant to 2 warmed plates. Pour sauce over.
Sprinkle 1 tablespoon of toasted pine nuts over each serving.

MAKES 2 SERVINGS
Each serving contains approximately:
   Calories: 520   *Cholesterol: 66 mg*
   Fat: 12 g   *Sodium: 513 mg*

How to Bone a Pheasant Breast with Wing Bone Attached

◆

This technique also works with chicken—or any other poultry.

1. Using a sharp boning or paring knife, loosen the skin from the breast pulling toward the wing bone.

4. Carefully cut breast meat away from the bone.

5. Use your knife to cut through the joint that connects the breast to the wing—without cutting through the meat.

8. Roll the breast around the pilaf as tightly as possible, rolling toward the wing.

9. Secure the roll by wrapping the wing bone around it.

2. Leave the skin intact on the wing bone.

3. Using scissors or kitchen shears, remove the loosened skin from the breast.

6. Spread the boned breast out flat.

7. Place ½ cup of pilaf (not shown here) in the center of the breast.

10. When cooked, the breast shrinks to reveal the pilaf.

Gingered Fruit Pilaf

This pilaf is easily "bulked up" for larger groups and is so good served cold as a rice salad that I always make enough to have leftovers.

½ teaspoon dark sesame oil
¼ cup brown rice
¼ cup chopped onion
½ cup defatted chicken stock
1 teaspoon sodium-reduced soy sauce
2 tablespoons sliced dried apricots
2 tablespoons sliced unsulfured dried apples
2 tablespoons raisins
½ teaspoon peeled and finely chopped fresh ginger

1. Preheat the oven to 400°F.

2. Heat the oil in a heavy skillet. Add the rice and onion and cook, stirring frequently, until browned, about 10 minutes.

3. Combine the stock and soy sauce in a saucepan and bring to a boil. Add to the rice mixture, then stir in all remaining ingredients. Spoon mixture into a baking dish. Cover tightly and bake for 45 minutes. Remove from oven and allow to stand for 10 minutes before removing cover.

MAKES TWO ½-CUP SERVINGS
Each serving contains approximately:
Calories: 166   Cholesterol: 0 mg
Fat: 2 g   Sodium: 126 mg

Pear Chutney

This chutney is used as an ingredient in the Curry Sauce, but it is also a wonderful condiment for fish, poultry or meat. I always double this recipe because it keeps beautifully and goes well with so many things.

4 cups dried unsulfured pears, diced
1 cup dried figs, finely diced
1 cup seedless raisins, finely diced
1 medium onion, finely chopped (1½ cups)
2 cups sugar
1¼ teaspoons ground ginger
¼ cup pickling spice, tied in a cheesecloth bag
2 cups water
2 cups cider vinegar

1. Combine all the ingredients in a large saucepan and bring to a boil. Reduce the heat and simmer slowly, uncovered, for 2 hours.

2. Cool to room temperature. Remove and discard the cheesecloth bag containing the spices. Refrigerate the chutney in a tightly covered container. It will keep for months.

MAKES 4¾ CUPS; NINETEEN ¼-CUP SERVINGS
Each serving contains approximately:
Calories: 175   Cholesterol: 0 mg
Fat: Negligible   Sodium: 10 mg

Frozen Lemon Cloud

A variation of the Frozen Key Lime Cloud on page 69, with raspberries and kiwis.

    1 egg, separated and yolk lightly beaten
    ¼ cup instant nonfat dry milk powder
    ¼ cup water
    2 tablespoons sugar
    ⅛ teaspoon finely grated lemon peel
    4 teaspoons fresh lemon juice
    1 kiwi, sliced, for garnish (optional)
      Raspberries, for garnish (optional)

1. Combine the egg white, milk powder, and water in a bowl and beat, using an electric mixer, until stiff peaks form.

2. Combine the egg yolk, sugar, lemon peel, and lemon juice. Mix well and slowly add to whipped mixture, continuing to beat.

3. Spoon 1 cup of the cloud carefully into each of 2 chilled bowls. Place in freezer until frozen. Before serving, top with kiwi slices and/or raspberries, if desired.

MAKES 2 SERVINGS

Each serving contains approximately:

Calories: 120 *Cholesterol: 108 mg*
Fat: 3 g *Sodium: 79 mg*

HOLIDAYS

Holidays offer the greatest challenge for lighter, lower-fat menu planning because they are all so steeped in tradition. And tradition always includes fabulous, rich recipes that have been handed down from generation to generation. The trick is to update these traditional recipes to be lower in fat, cholesterol, and sodium without losing any of the taste, texture, and appearance that made them so coveted in the first place. This challenge makes planning lighter holiday menus even more fun, and you will get both high marks and rave reviews from your appreciative guests.

Traditional Thanksgiving

❖

Williamsburg Onion Soup

Holiday Waldorf Salad

Roast Turkey with Fresh Marjoram
and Light Turkey-Mushroom Gravy

Cornbread Dressing

Mashed Potatoes (page 73)

Scalloped Sweet Potatoes

Herbed Green Beans

Cranberry Relish

"Winter" Fruit Compote
with Cinnamon-Yogurt Sauce

Pumpkin Tarts

Of all American holidays, Thanksgiving is by far the most specifically food related. After all, it is a celebration of that first "feast" giving thanks for a new homeland and its abundance.

Thanksgiving dinner is traditionally served family style, with all of the side dishes in serving bowls on the table. The turkey is usually carved at the table and each guest chooses his or her favorite part of the bird. This manner of serving makes the meal more relaxed and informal. Foods are not expected to be piping hot. Indeed, food historians tell us, in colonial times all food was served closer to room temperature. Keeping this in mind, cooking and serving this Thanksgiving meal should be easy and lots of fun.

The most exciting and surprising part of this truly traditional Thanksgiving menu is that the entire meal contains about 1,000 calories and only 20 percent of those calories are from fat and less than 10 percent are from saturated fat. Both the cholesterol and sodium contents of this hearty and satisfying holiday repast are enough to make the American Heart Association jump for joy.

WILLIAMSBURG ONION SOUP

I first tasted this soup at an International Food Media Conference in Washington, D.C. A dinner from colonial America was presented by the Colonial Williamsburg Foundation, and we were given recipes for all of the dishes served. I could not believe that a soup this delicious was made with water, and I couldn't wait to get home and try it for myself. To my amazement the results were equally tasty and I was able to lighten it up a considerable amount without losing any of the hearty taste and texture. The original recipe is from *The Art of Cookery Made Plain and Easy,* by Hannah Glasse, published in 1747. I've included Hannah's original recipe (page 136).

Williamsburg Onion Soup.

¼ cup corn oil margarine

4 large onions (2 pounds), finely diced (6 cups)

1 tablespoon flour

1½ teaspoons salt

4½ cups water, boiling

1 cup stale whole wheat bread crumbs

1 egg yolk

2 teaspoons cider vinegar

1. In a heavy saucepan over low heat, melt the margarine, add the onions, and sauté, stirring frequently, for 15 to 20 minutes or until very soft.

2. Add the flour and salt and continue cooking, stirring constantly, for 2 more minutes. *Do not brown!* Add the boiling water and mix well. Add the bread crumbs, mix well, and simmer for 10 minutes uncovered, stirring frequently.

3. Remove from heat. Combine the egg yolk and vinegar, then stir about ⅓ cup of the hot soup into the egg and vinegar. Stir egg mixture back into soup, mix well, and serve.

MAKES EIGHT ¾-CUP SERVINGS

Each serving contains approximately:

Calories: 153   Cholesterol: 27 mg

Fat: 7 g   Sodium: 618 mg

HOLIDAY WALDORF SALAD

I particularly like a Waldorf salad because it adds a wonderfully crunchy texture to any menu. My version varies from tradition in that I have eliminated the mayonnaise and, thus, the cholesterol. Since there is no dairy product in this recipe, it is perfectly kosher to serve to any of your guests with their turkey.

I always make more of this salad than I plan to serve with my holiday meal. I add leftover cooked turkey to it and serve it as an entree salad for lunch the next day. It keeps well and is always a crowd pleaser. Also, I often substitute diced fresh fennel bulb for half the celery. It adds an unusual and pleasant licorice taste to the salad.

DRESSING

1 cup silken soft tofu

½ teaspoon salt

1 teaspoon sugar

¾ teaspoon curry powder

¼ teaspoon ground cinnamon

⅛ teaspoon ground ginger

1 tablespoon fresh lemon juice

1 tablespoon canola or corn oil

1 cup coarsely chopped raw almonds

3 cups diced celery, without leaves

4 red Delicious apples (2 pounds), cored
and diced (6 cups)

½ cup chopped chives or green onion
tops (½-inch pieces)

½ cup raisins

1. If possible, make the dressing several hours or the day before you intend to serve it. Combine all dressing ingredients in a food processor and blend until satin smooth. (Makes 1 cup.)

2. Toast the chopped almonds in a preheated 350°F. oven for 8 to 10 minutes or until lightly browned. Watch carefully, as they burn easily. Set aside.

3. Combine the celery, apples, chives or green onions, and raisins in a large bowl. Add the dressing and toss until thoroughly mixed.

4. Place ½ cup of salad on each of 8 chilled plates and top each salad with 1 tablespoon toasted almonds. (If you do not use all of this salad, keep the remaining almonds separate to sprinkle over the leftover salad when it is served.)

MAKES SIXTEEN ½-CUP SERVINGS

Each serving contains approximately:

Calories: 115   Cholesterol: 0 mg
Fat: 6 g   Sodium: 97 mg

Roast Turkey with Fresh Marjoram and Light Turkey-Mushroom Gravy

◆

No Thanksgiving would be complete without the traditional turkey to carve. This is one of my favorite methods for roasting turkey. By turning it from one side to the other during the roasting time, the turkey is far more moist. And defatting the turkey drippings not only makes a healthier gravy, it also is the best looking and most flavorful you've ever tasted. Nobody likes greasy gravy!

12- to 15-pound turkey

3 medium onions, peeled and quartered
(1½ pounds)

½ cup fresh marjoram

½ cup chopped fresh parsley

2 cups defatted chicken stock

LIGHT TURKEY-MUSHROOM GRAVY

1 to 4 cups defatted Chicken Stock
(page 40)

3 tablespoons cornstarch

¼ cup water

1 teaspoon corn oil margarine

1 cup sliced fresh mushrooms (¼ pound)

½ teaspoon salt

¼ teaspoon freshly ground black pepper

1. Preheat the oven to 325°F. Wash the turkey inside and out and pat dry. Stuff the turkey with the onions, marjoram, and parsley. Using metal skewers, pin the ends of the turkey wings together and close the cavity of the bird. Tie the wings together with string. Truss the turkey at the cavity to close the opening tightly. Tie the legs together.

2. Place turkey on its side on a rack in a roasting pan. Pour the stock over the top and roast, uncovered, for approximately 20 minutes per pound, basting every 15 or 20 minutes.

3. Halfway through the cooking, turn the turkey on its other side. If the turkey starts to get too brown, cover it with a lid of foil.

4. Remove the turkey from the oven. Transfer it to a platter and allow it to rest for 20 minutes before carving.

5. Transfer the turkey drippings from the pan to a bowl and place in the freezer. As soon as the fat has congealed on top, skim off the fat.

6. In a saucepan, place the defatted turkey drippings and enough chicken stock to equal 4 cups. Bring to a boil, then dissolve the cornstarch in the water and add to the gravy. Reduce heat and simmer, stirring occasionally, until mixture thickens slightly.

7. While the gravy is cooking, heat the margarine in a skillet and add the mushrooms. Cook, covered, until tender, about 3 minutes. Add mushrooms to the gravy along with salt and pepper and mix well. (Makes 3 cups.)

8. Remove the skin from the turkey before serving along with the gravy.

MAKES 25 TO 30 SERVINGS
Each serving 3.5 ounces, light and dark meat, without skin and gravy contains approximately:

Calories: 175   Cholesterol: 75 mg
Fat: 6 g   Sodium: 70 mg

GRAVY
Eight ⅓ cup servings
Each serving contains approximately:

Calories: 42   Cholesterol: Negligible
Fat: 2 g   Sodium: 212 mg

CORNBREAD DRESSING

Everyone has his or her favorite turkey dressing and this is mine. It is also easy to make and can be assembled ahead of time and baked just before serving. I never stuff the bird with the dressing because the turkey fat saturates the stuffing and the turkey will keep longer if not stuffed.

>   3 cups cornbread, crumbled (½ recipe
>   page 156)
>   2 slices whole wheat bread, toasted and
>   crumbled
> 1½ teaspoons ground sage
>   ½ teaspoon freshly ground black pepper
>   1 tablespoon corn oil margarine
>   1 medium onion, finely chopped (1½
>   cups)
> 1½ cups chopped celery
>   ½ cup chopped fresh parsley
>   2 cups defatted chicken stock

1. Preheat the oven to 350°F.

2. Combine the cornbread, toast, sage, and pepper in a large bowl and mix well.

3. Melt the margarine in a skillet. Add the onion, celery, and parsley, and sauté until vegetables are tender, about 15 to 20 minutes.

4. Add the vegetables to the dry ingredients and mix well. Add stock and again mix well.

5. Spoon the dressing into a baking dish or casserole (8 x 8 x 2 or 9 x 9 x 1½ or 9 x 5 x 3) and bake uncovered for 45 minutes.

MAKES TWELVE ½-CUP SERVINGS
Each serving contains approximately:
Calories: 91   Cholesterol: Negligible
Fat: 3 g   Sodium: 231 mg

NOTE: This recipe can be made with all whole wheat bread if desired.

SCALLOPED SWEET POTATOES

Rather than the more usual candied yam casserole for Thanksgiving, I prefer the natural sweetness of these scalloped sweet potatoes. I sometimes use yams for this delightfully different recipe because they are more colorful than sweet potatoes. Sometimes, I combine yams and sweet potatoes for a two-tone presentation.

>   3 or 4 sweet potatoes (2 pounds), peeled
>   and thinly sliced (6 cups)
>   1 tablespoon flour
>   ½ teaspoon freshly grated nutmeg
>   ¼ teaspoon salt
>   ⅛ teaspoon cayenne pepper
>   2 large leeks, white part only,
>   thinly sliced (1 cup)
> 1½ teaspoons corn oil margarine
>   1 cup 2% low-fat milk

1. Preheat the oven to 350°F. Coat a 2-quart flat baking dish with nonstick vegetable spray.

2. Layer 2 cups of the sweet potatoes in the bottom of the dish and sprinkle with half the flour, nutmeg, salt, and cayenne pepper. Top with ½ cup of leeks.

3. Repeat with 2 more cups sweet potatoes. Sprinkle with remaining flour, nutmeg, salt, and cayenne. Top with remaining leeks.

4. Layer remaining sweet potatoes evenly over the top. Dot with margarine and pour the milk over the top. Bake, uncovered, for 45 minutes or until the potatoes can be pierced easily with a fork. Remove from oven. Before serving, allow to rest 10 minutes or until liquid is absorbed.

MAKES EIGHT ¼-CUP SERVINGS
Each serving contains approximately:
Calories: 80   Cholesterol: 2 mg
Fat: 1 g   Sodium: 105 mg

My Thanksgiving spread, clockwise from top left: Herbed Green Beans, Mashed Potatoes, Cranberry Relish, Roast Turkey, and Cornbread Dressing.

HERBED GREEN BEANS

1 pound fresh green beans (4 cups)
2 tablespoons canola or corn oil
1 tablespoon fresh basil, finely chopped,
    or 1 teaspoon dried, crushed with
    mortar and pestle
¼ teaspoon salt
¼ cup finely chopped fresh parsley
¼ cup finely chopped chives or green
    onion tops

1. Steam the green beans for 5 minutes. Rinse under cold running water, drain, and set aside.

2. In a large skillet, heat the oil. Add the basil, salt, parsley, and chives and mix well. Add the beans and mix thoroughly. Heat just to serving temperature.

MAKES EIGHT ½-CUP SERVINGS
Each serving contains approximately:
Calories: 55   Cholesterol: 0 mg
Fat: 4 g   Sodium: 77 mg

CRANBERRY RELISH

The perfect accompaniment for this fabulous fowl is this tart cranberry relish. The gelatin is added only to firm it up a bit and can easily be eliminated. I particularly like the crunchiness added by the celery, and cutting it in crescents enhances the appearance of the sauce.

1 envelope unflavored gelatin
2 tablespoons cool water
½ cup unsweetened frozen apple juice
    concentrate, undiluted, boiling
3 stalks celery
    Zest of 1 orange (1 tablespoon)
    Zest of 1 lemon (1 teaspoon)
1 teaspoon fresh lemon juice
2 large oranges, peeled, all membranes
    removed, finely diced
½ pound fresh or frozen cranberries,
    coarsely chopped or left whole, as
    desired
1 cup fresh or thawed frozen
    raspberries, pureed
1 cup unsweetened applesauce

1. Soften the gelatin in the cool water. Add the boiling apple juice concentrate and stir until completely dissolved. Set aside.

2. Cut the leaves and white ends off each stalk of celery. Remove any large strings. Chop crosswise thinly to create crescents.

3. Combine the gelatin mixture, celery, and all other ingredients; mix well. Pour into a 1½-quart serving dish and cover tightly. Store in the refrigerator until gelled.

MAKES SIXTEEN ¼-CUP SERVINGS
Each serving contains approximately:
Calories: 43   Cholesterol: 0 mg
Fat: Negligible   Sodium: 6 mg

TURKEY SOUP

Turkey leftovers are a strong part of the holiday tradition in most American homes. For this reason I have included my own favorite turkey leftover recipe, which is a hearty and truly tasty turkey soup.

1 turkey carcass
1 medium onion, quartered
1 medium carrot, scraped and chopped
2 bay leaves
½ teaspoon dried basil, crushed
¼ teaspoon dried thyme, crushed
¼ teaspoon dried marjoram, crushed
1 teaspoon salt
¼ teaspoon black peppercorns
    Leftover turkey drippings or gravy
½ cup rice
2 stalks celery, finely chopped
2 tablespoons corn oil margarine
3 cups sliced fresh mushrooms
3 cups chopped cooked turkey, skin
    removed
3 tablespoons Madeira

1. Break up the turkey carcass and put in an 8- to 10-quart pot or soup kettle. Add vegetables, herbs, seasonings, and drippings. Add enough cold water to cover by at least 1 inch. Cover, leaving the lid ajar to allow the steam to escape, and simmer slowly for 4 hours.

2. Cool to room temperature and refrigerate, uncovered, overnight. When the fat has hardened on the surface, remove and discard.

3. Warm the stock until it becomes liquid. Strain the liquid, discarding carcass and vegetables, and pour it back into the pot and bring to a boil.

4. Add the rice and celery and cook for 30 minutes.

5. Melt the margarine in a skillet and sauté the mushrooms until they are just tender, about 3 minutes. Add the mushrooms and the diced turkey to the soup and cook for another 30 minutes. Just before serving, add the Madeira.

**MAKES AT LEAST
EIGHT ¾-CUP SERVINGS**
Each serving contains approximately:
Calories: 145   Cholesterol: 47 mg
Fat: 5 g   Sodium: 101 mg

NOTE: Add any leftover turkey dressing to your soup.

"WINTER" FRUIT COMPOTE

In the late autumn and winter, when fresh fruit is either not available or very pricey, dried fruits offer an excellent and naturally sweet alternative for snacks, sauces, and desserts. This compote is a wonderfully light and tangy dessert after a larger than usual holiday meal. I particularly like it served with Cinnamon-Yogurt Sauce spooned over the top.

> 1½ *tablespoons peeled and finely
>   chopped fresh ginger*
> 2¼ *cups water*
>   1 *cup (6 ounces) dried apricots,
>   chopped*
> 1½ *cups (4 ounces) dried apple slices,
>   halved*
>   ¼ *cup currants or raisins*

1. Place the ginger in a saucepan and cover with 3 to 4 inches of water. Bring to a boil and cook, uncovered, for 15 minutes. Drain and set aside.

2. Combine the water, apricots, and apples in another pot and bring to a boil. Reduce heat and simmer, covered, for 25 minutes or until tender.

3. Add the ginger and currants or raisins to the fruit mixture. Cool to room temperature, cover, and refrigerate for several hours or overnight.

Our two desserts: "Winter" Fruit Compote and Pumpkin Tart.

4. Remove from refrigerator and bring to room temperature. Serve with Cinnamon-Yogurt Sauce (recipe follows).

**MAKES TWELVE ¼-CUP SERVINGS
(WITHOUT SAUCE)**
Each serving contains approximately:
Calories: 60   Cholesterol: 0 mg
Fat: Negligible   Sodium: 7 mg

CINNAMON-YOGURT SAUCE

This sauce is also marvelous on the Pumpkin Tarts. When serving more than one dessert, I like to serve a sauce that works for all of them. Your guests may choose one or the other—or in the true spirit of this food-indulgent holiday, they may well choose to have both!

>   2 *cups plain nonfat yogurt*
>   ½ *cup unsweetened frozen apple juice
>   concentrate, undiluted*
>   1 *tablespoon vanilla extract*
>   1 *teaspoon ground cinnamon*

Combine all the ingredients and mix well. Refrigerate in a tightly covered container.

**MAKES 2½ CUPS; TWENTY-FOUR
2-TABLESPOON SERVINGS**
Each serving contains approximately:
Calories: 23   Cholesterol: Negligible
Fat: Negligible   Sodium: 40 mg

PUMPKIN TARTS

Phyllo tart shells win in all categories over regular pie crust. They are prettier, lower in fat and calories, and easier to make. The filling in these tarts is also the fastest and easiest ever—and absolutely delicious.

FILLING

2 cups mashed cooked pumpkin (1 16-ounce can)
2 cups low-fat ricotta cheese
¼ cup sugar
1 tablespoon ground cinnamon
1 teaspoon ground allspice
¼ teaspoon fresh grated nutmeg
4 teaspoons vanilla extract

SHELLS

8 sheets phyllo dough
Nonstick vegetable spray

Ground cinnamon

1. Combine the filling ingredients in a food processor with a metal blade and blend until *satin* smooth. Refrigerate, covered, several hours or overnight.

2. Preheat the oven to 350°F. Trim the edges off 8 sheets of phyllo dough to form a square, discarding the remnants. Quarter the resulting squares to form 4 piles of 8 sheets each; you now have 32 small squares.

3. Place 1 square of phyllo dough on the counter, coat with nonstick vegetable spray, and dust lightly with cinnamon. Place a second square on top of the first square, fanning the squares so that all corners are separated from those that have come before. Continue in this way until you have built up 4 layers—this is one tart shell. Repeat to create 8 tart shells.

4. Coat 2 baking sheets with nonstick vegetable spray. Arrange eight ½-cup ramekins or custard cups, inverted, on top of the baking sheets and coat each ramekin with nonstick vegetable spray. Place one tart shell on top of each inverted ramekin. Press down onto sides of cup. Note: Be sure edges of dough do not overlap or touch, as this will cause them to stick and break when you remove them from the ramekins after baking.

5. Bake for about 12 minutes or until golden brown. Remove from oven, cool slightly, and lift each phyllo shell off the cup, placing it right side up on a serving dish or individual plates. Spoon or pipe ½ cup of pumpkin filling mixture into each tart shell.

MAKES 8 SERVINGS
Each serving contains approximately:
Calories: 197   Cholesterol: 19 mg
Fat: 5 g   Sodium: 156 mg

HOW TO MAKE PUMPKIN TARTS

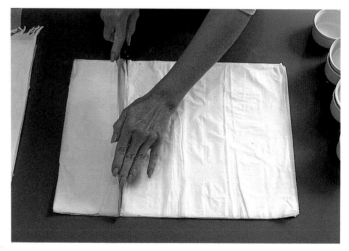

1. Stack 8 sheets of phyllo dough and trim to form a square. Quarter the large square; you now have 32 small squares, or 4 stacks of 8 squares each.

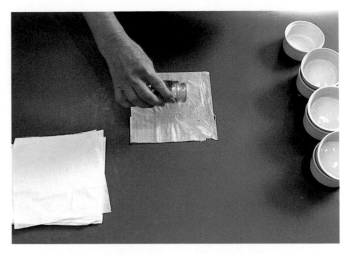

2. Coat one square with nonstick vegetable spray.

3. Dust with cinnamon.

4. Coating and dusting each square as you go, stack the squares, fanning them so that all the corners show.

5. Place each stack on top of an inverted ramekin. which has been coated with nonstick vegetable spray, and press down on the sides of the cup.

6. Put the ramekins on a baking sheet that you have coated with nonstick vegetable spray, making sure that tart shells do not touch one another. Bake.

7. Cool slightly and lift each tart shell off of the ramekin. Place the tart shell right side up on a serving dish and fill with pumpkin filling.

Christmas Cocktail Party

❖

Caviar Cocktail Crepes

Savory Polenta Squares

*Gift-Wrapped Sausages
with Herbed Mustard Sauce*

Cocktail Duck Quesadillas

Cocktail Salmon Tamales

This holiday season, when you start making your Christmas gift list, include for yourself a slimmer waistline and a shaplier body. Tradition is a wonderful thing, but it does not have to dictate calorie by calorie exactly how each dish is to be made. Lighter, low-fat ingredients can be substituted amazingly well in recipes for most of the seasonal favorites.

Christmas carols and champagne set the scene for this festive Christmas Cocktail Party. The hors d'oeuvres feature a selection of tasty tidbits all designed in the red and green colors of the season. Also, all of these hors d'oeuvres can easily be quadrupled for lunch or dinner entrees.

CAVIAR COCKTAIL CREPES

You can use any type of caviar you like to make these crepes. For holiday parties I like salmon caviar best because of its color. For an entree, make larger dilled crepes and fill them with the mixture for Salmon Tamales (page 151), but sauté the salmon with the onions, then garnish the crepes with this "cream" and caviar. This basic fat-free crepe can be used for other recipes too, with or without the dill, or seasoned with other herbs or spices.

FILLING

1 cup low-fat ricotta cheese
1 tablespoon fresh lemon juice

24 Dilled Crepes (recipe follows)
3 tablespoons caviar, preferably salmon
24 chives, blanched

1. Combine the filling ingredients in a food processor with a metal blade and blend until satin-smooth.

2. Spoon 2 teaspoons filling on each crepe. Top with ½ teaspoon caviar and roll crepe closed.

3. Tie each rolled crepe with a chive.

MAKES 24 CREPES
Each crepe contains approximately:
Calories: 39   *Cholesterol: 15 mg*
Fat: 1 g   *Sodium: 78 mg*

DILLED CREPES

¾ cup whole wheat flour
¼ teaspoon salt
½ teaspoon dried dill, crushed
1 cup nonfat (skim) milk
2 egg whites
  Nonstick vegetable spray

1. Combine the flour, salt, and dill and mix well. Add the milk and beat with an egg beater until well mixed. Add the egg whites and oil and continue beating until well mixed.

2. Heat a crepe pan until a drop of water dances on the surface. Coat the surface with nonstick vegetable spray and wipe out using a paper towel. Spoon 1 tablespoon of batter in the center of the pan. When the edges start to curl, turn the crepe and brown the other side, about 3 minutes total. Place the crepes in a covered container as you make them to keep them pliable.

MAKES 24 COCKTAIL CREPES
Each crepe contains approximately:
Calories: 19   *Cholesterol: Negligible*
Fat: Negligible   *Sodium: 34 mg*

NOTE: To freeze crepes, separate with pieces of aluminum foil or wax paper. Wrap tightly and place in the freezer. (Before using frozen crepes, thaw to room temperature and place in preheated 300°F. oven for 20 minutes or until soft and pliable.)

SAVORY POLENTA SQUARES

These are good served hot, cold, or at room temperature. I serve them here at room temperature, but if they are an appetizer or entree, I serve them hot and use the Perfect Red Pepper Soup on page 102 as a sauce.

½ cup yellow grits
1½ cups defatted Chicken Stock
  (page 40)
1 garlic clove, pressed or minced
2 ounces goat cheese, crumbled (½ cup)
¼ cup dry sun-dried tomatoes (not in
  oil), julienned (I use scissors)

1. Combine the grits and ½ cup of the stock and set aside.

2. Bring the remaining cup of stock to a boil in a heavy pan. Add the garlic and moistened grits, stirring constantly. Reduce heat to a simmer, cover, and cook for 20 minutes, stirring occasionally. Remove from heat and add the cheese and tomatoes. Mix until all cheese has melted and all ingredients are well blended.

3. Spoon the polenta into a 9 x 5-inch loaf pan that has been coated with nonstick vegetable spray. Press down evenly over the bottom. Allow to cool to room temperature. Cover and refrigerate until cold before serving for hors d'oeuvre.

4. Invert polenta onto a cutting board and cut into 32 squares.

MAKES 32 SQUARES
Each square contains approximately:
Calories: 10   *Cholesterol: 2 mg*
Fat: Negligible   *Sodium: 20 mg*

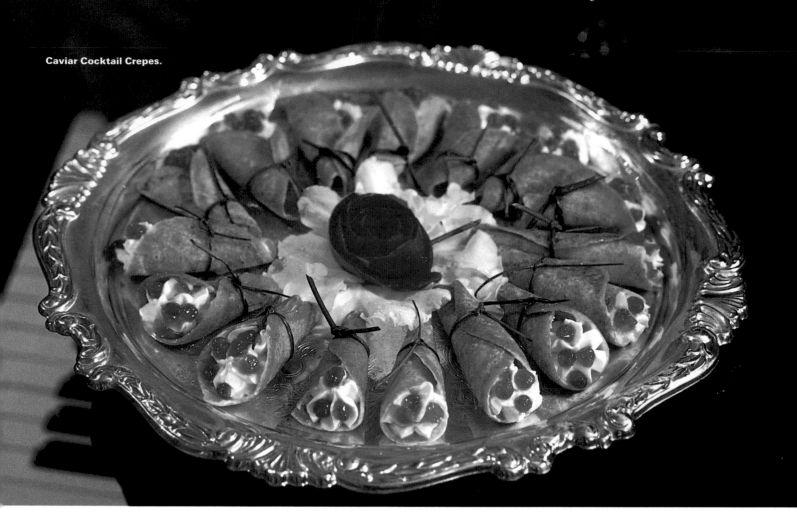

Caviar Cocktail Crepes.

Savory Polenta Squares.

Gift-Wrapped Sausages

These little gift-wrapped sausages are always a conversation piece at parties. They are festive-looking and awfully tasty. I especially like them dipped in this mustard sauce. The sauce is also good on fish, poultry, or meat and can be used as a salad dressing.

A larger version of this sausage makes a truly dramatic appetizer or entree. Follow the directions for making the phyllo crust for the Cinnamon-Apple Wonder on page 108, but fill it with a 4-ounce cooked sausage pattie instead.

SAUSAGE
    1 pound lean ground turkey or chicken
1½ teaspoons dried sage, crushed
    ½ teaspoon mace
    ½ teaspoon garlic powder
    ½ teaspoon freshly ground black pepper
    ¼ teaspoon salt
    ⅛ teaspoon ground allspice
    ⅛ teaspoon ground cloves
    ½ cup defatted Chicken Stock (page 40)
    6 sheets phyllo dough
   32 chives, blanched

1. Combine the sausage ingredients in a bowl and mix well.

2. Divide the mixture into 32 (1¼ inch) balls. Pour the stock into a large skillet and bring to a boil. Add the sausage balls and cook, covered, for 5 minutes. Remove sausage balls and place on paper towels to drain.

3. Preheat the oven to 350°F. Spread one sheet of phyllo dough on a countertop and coat with nonstick vegetable spray. Cover with another sheet of phyllo and spray again. (Keep unused phyllo dough covered with a damp towel as you work to prevent its drying out.) Cut the phyllo sheets into 12 four-inch squares. Place one sausage ball in the center of each square and bring the 4 corners together to form a package. Twist to seal and lightly coat again with nonstick vegetable spray. Repeat with the remaining dough and sausage.

4. Place all packages on a baking sheet that has been coated with nonstick vegetable spray. Bake for about 12 minutes, or until phyllo is a golden brown. Remove from oven and tie each package with a blanched chive.

5. Serve as an hors d'oeuvre with a bowl of Herbed Mustard Sauce (page 149) on the side for dipping.

MAKES 32 PACKAGES
Each package contains approximately:

Calories: 35   Cholesterol: 9 mg
Fat: 1 g   Sodium: 44 mg

HERBED MUSTARD SAUCE

1 cup silken soft tofu
1 tablespoon fresh lemon juice
2 tablespoons Dijon mustard
¼ teaspoon fresh thyme leaves, or crushed dried
¼ teaspoon fresh rosemary leaves, or crushed dried
¼ teaspoon salt
⅛ teaspoon freshly ground black pepper
1 garlic clove, chopped
1½ teaspoons extra-virgin olive oil

Combine all ingredients in a blender container and blend until satin-smooth.

MAKES 1 CUP
Each tablespoon contains approximately:

Calories: 14   Cholesterol: 0 mg
Fat: 1 g   Sodium: 51 mg

COCKTAIL DUCK QUESADILLAS

Cocktail quesadillas are marvelous finger food for parties. You can substitute any leftover fish, poultry, or meat for the duck—or they're good without any meat at all. If you want a hotter quesadilla, substitute jalapeño peppers for the green chilies, or add cayenne pepper or Tabasco. To make larger, entree-size quesadillas, use the whole tortilla and quadruple the filling ingredients.

12 whole wheat tortillas
¼ cup grated 20% fat-reduced Monterey Jack cheese
¼ pound cooked duck breast, skin removed and julienned (1 cup)
1 (4-ounce) can chopped green chilies
1 (4-ounce) jar sliced pimientos
½ cup finely chopped onion

1. Using a cookie cutter, cup, or water glass as a pattern, cut three 3-inch circles from each of the 12 tortillas. (Freeze remaining tortilla scraps to use in casseroles.)

2. Top each tortilla with 1 tablespoon grated cheese, 3 strips julienned duck breast, and ¾ teaspoon each of the chilies, pimientos, and onion.

3. Place a few quesadillas in a large skillet that has been coated with nonstick vegetable spray. Cook over medium heat until cheese has melted. Fold each quesadilla in half and lightly brown on both sides. Repeat with remaining quesadillas.

MAKES 36 QUESADILLAS
Each quesadilla contains approximately:

Calories: 55   Cholesterol: 4 mg
Fat: 2 g   Sodium: 45 mg

Cocktail Duck Quesadillas.

COCKTAIL SALMON TAMALES

The idea for these tamales came from Vincent Guerithault, the chef and owner of Vincent's on Camelback, a wonderful restaurant in Scottsdale, Arizona. Vincent demonstrated his technique for making cocktail-size tamales at an American Cuisine Conference in Santa Fe. I was so impressed with his tamales that I immediately started working on my own. To serve these tamales as an entree, simply make each tamale four times as big. Masa harina is available in the flour section of any large supermarket.

FILLING

½ medium onion, finely diced (¾ cup)
½ cup diced raw salmon
1 tablespoon chopped canned green chilies
1 tablespoon chopped cilantro (fresh coriander)
¼ teaspoon salt
¼ teaspoon freshly ground black pepper

TAMALES

1½ cups masa harina
½ teaspoon salt
½ teaspoon freshly ground black pepper
½ teaspoon paprika
¼ teaspoon ground cumin
¼ teaspoon cayenne pepper
¾ cup warm water
2 tablespoons canola or corn oil
1 tablespoon light sour cream
15 corn husks, halved crosswise, for garnish

1. To make the filling, sweat the onion in a covered nonstick skillet over low heat just until soft, about 15 to 20 minutes. Add a little water if necessary to prevent scorching. Combine the onion with remaining filling ingredients and mix well. Set aside.

2. To make tamales, combine the dry ingredients and mix well. Combine the water and oil and add to the dry ingredients. Blend until smooth. Blend in the sour cream and knead as you would bread dough.

3. Divide dough into 30 (1¼-inches in diameter) balls. Press each ball flat between 2 pieces of wax paper and smooth out into a circle 3 inches in diameter with your fingers.

4. Remove the piece of wax paper on top and place 1 rounded teaspoon of the filling mixture in the center of each circle of dough. Using the bottom sheet of paper, lift and fold one edge of the dough over the top of the filling. Repeat with the other edge of the dough to make a tubular envelope and press firmly to seal the dough tightly around the filling. It is necessary to use new wax paper each time to prevent sticking.

5. Roll each tamale in plastic wrap and twist each end firmly to round and seal ends. Steam the tamales over rapidly boiling water for 10 minutes.

6. Unwrap the tamales and place each in a halved corn husk tied with a ribbon or a strip of husk.

MAKES 30 APPROXIMATELY 2-INCH-LONG COCKTAIL TAMALES

Each tamale contains approximately:
Calories: 37   Cholesterol: 2 mg
Fat: 1 g   Sodium: 66 mg

Turnip Salad.

2 teaspoons thyme, crushed
2½ teaspoons salt
1 teaspoon sugar
½ teaspoon freshly ground black pepper
½ teaspoon crushed red pepper

Combine drained black-eyed peas and all ingredients and bring to a boil. Reduce heat and simmer, covered, for about 2 hours, or until peas are tender.

MAKES SIXTEEN 1-CUP SERVINGS

Each serving contains approximately:
Calories: 220   Cholesterol: 0 mg
Fat: 1 g   Sodium: 230 mg

NOTE: If black-eyed peas have not been soaked overnight, combine them with the 12 cups water, bring to a boil, and boil for 2 minutes. Remove from heat and allow to stand for 1 hour then add remaining ingredients and cook for about 2 hours or until peas are tender.

BLACK-EYED PEA CASSEROLE

This is the ultimate party dish. It is very inexpensive, very easy to make, and can be left out for hours without spoiling. It is also really tasty and *lucky*! In this vegetarian menu it is served with cornbread to combine a legume (bean) with a grain (corn) for complete protein. If you prefer, serve it over rice or as a side dish with fish, poultry, or meat.

2 pounds dried black-eyed peas
  (6 cups) soaked overnight and
  drained (see Note)
12 cups water
2 (6-ounce) cans tomato paste
½ cup red wine vinegar
2 medium onions, chopped (3 cups)
4 garlic cloves, pressed or peeled and
  minced
2 green bell peppers, seeded and
  chopped
4 medium carrots, peeled and chopped
4 large tomatoes, chopped or
  1 (26-ounce) can whole tomatoes,
  drained and chopped
2 teaspoons oregano, crushed

MUSTARD GREENS WITH PEPPERED VINEGAR

Mustard greens brighten any buffet with their brilliant green color. (Turnip or collard greens may also be used.) Overcooking will dull their hue and make them bitter, so watch them carefully. The peppered vinegar adds zing to these healthful greens.

½ cup small dried peppers
1 cup cider vinegar
10 bunches mustard greens (8 pounds)

1. Place peppers in a bottle. Add vinegar and allow to stand for at least 24 hours before using.

2. Soak greens in cold water to loosen any attached dirt or grit and wash thoroughly. Remove any large, tough veins. Steam greens until limp and bright green, about 2 minutes. (You can also do the greens in a microwave.) Serve with Peppered Vinegar.

MAKES SIXTEEN ¾-CUP SERVINGS

Each serving contains approximately:
Calories: 17   Cholesterol: 0 mg
Fat: Negligible   Sodium: 17 mg

Black-Eyed Pea Casserole.

Mustard Greens with Peppered Vinegar.

CORNBREAD STICKS

I like to make the cornbread sticks in corn molds because they look so much fancier for a party. However, this recipe works just as well made in an 8-inch pan and cut into sixteen 2-inch squares.

1 cup yellow cornmeal
1 cup whole wheat flour
3 tablespoons sugar
4 teaspoons baking powder
½ teaspoon salt
2 egg whites, lightly beaten
2 tablespoons corn oil
1 cup nonfat (skim) milk
1 teaspoon vanilla extract

1. Preheat the oven to 400°F. Combine the cornmeal, flour, sugar, baking powder, and salt. Mix well.

2. In another bowl combine the egg whites, corn oil, milk, and vanilla, and mix well.

3. Pour the liquid ingredients into the dry ingredients, and mix until the liquid is absorbed. Do not overmix.

4. Fill 16 corn-stick molds or small muffin tins, and bake for 17 minutes.

MAKES 16 STICKS

Each stick contains approximately:
Calories: 86   Cholesterol: Negligible
Fat: 2 g   Sodium: 256 mg

PECAN PUDDING

◆

This pudding is a lower-calorie, custardlike version of a praline and just as delicious. If you are preparing a strict vegetarian menu, then it must be made with agar-agar instead of gelatin.

  2 cups pecan halves (½ pound)
  2 envelopes unflavored gelatin
  4 tablespoons water
  5 cups nonfat (skim) milk
  ½ cup corn oil margarine
  1½ cups packed dark brown sugar
  4 teaspoons vanilla extract

1. Preheat the oven to 350°F. Coarsely chop 1 cup of the pecans and leave remaining cup in halves. Place all pecans in oven for 8 to 10 minutes or until browned, keeping the chopped nuts separate from the halved ones. Watch carefully, as they burn easily. Set aside.

2. Add the water to the gelatin and allow to soften.

3. Combine milk, margarine, and sugar in a saucepan and cook over medium heat, stirring constantly with a wire whisk. Just before mixture comes to a boil, immediately remove from heat. (If allowed to boil, mixture will separate and have a grainy appearance. This does not ruin the taste, but it does detract from the appearance.) Add vanilla and gelatin and mix well. Allow to cool to room temperature and pour ½ cup in each of 16 ramekins or custard cups. Add 1 tablespoon of toasted chopped pecans to each dish and mix well. (They will rise back to the top.) Arrange 5 pecan halves on the top of each serving for garnish. Refrigerate for at least 4 hours before serving. (If you do not have small ramekins, pour mixture into a large casserole or soufflé dish. Add the chopped pecans, reserving the whole pecans to garnish individual servings when scooped into serving bowls.)

MAKES SIXTEEN ½-CUP SERVINGS
Each serving contains approximately:
Calories: 262   Cholesterol: 7 mg
Fat: 15 g   Sodium: 286 mg

St. Patrick's Day Potatoes on Parade

❖

Caviar Cocktail Bon Bons

Vichyssoise in a Spud Bowl

Potato Salad in Potato Rings

Irish Lamb Stew Stuffed Spuds

*Twice-Baked Potato and
Raisin Pudding*

Outrageous is the first word that always comes to mind when I'm planning a St. Patrick's Day party. And it well describes this St. Patrick's Day party menu: Potatoes on Parade. Everything from soup to dessert is served in a potato—and all accompanied by a pint of green beer! Just the luck o' the Irish, all of the potatoes for this menu can be baked at the same time, which saves both time and energy.

Caviar Cocktail Bon Bons.

CAVIAR COCKTAIL BON BONS

These bon bons are ideal bite-size hors d'oeuvres for any occasion, certainly the perfect appetizer for this stuffed-spud Irish feast.

24 small new potatoes, washed and dried
¼ cup caviar (your favorite or whatever your budget will allow)

1. Preheat the oven to 400°F. Bake the potatoes for 45 minutes. Remove from the oven and cool on a rack until comfortable to handle.

2. Using a melon baller, remove a scoop from the top of each potato. Fill each depression with about ½ teaspoon of caviar.

MAKES 24 BON BONS
Each bon bon contains approximately:
Calories: 73   Cholesterol: 16 mg
Fat: 1 g   Sodium: 45 mg

VICHYSSOISE IN A SPUD BOWL

This vichyssoise is a variation on the fabulous cold soup served for the Black and White After-the-Theater Supper. Both recipes are made with onions and potatoes rather than leeks, and both derive their creaminess from skim milk and light sour cream rather than heavy cream.

6 (12-ounce) baking potatoes
½ cup chopped onion
¾ cup defatted Chicken Stock (page 40)
¼ cup nonfat (skim) milk
¼ cup light sour cream
¼ teaspoon salt (omit if using salted stock)
⅛ teaspoon freshly ground black pepper
1 teaspoon fresh lemon juice
Chopped chives, for garnish (optional)

1. Preheat the oven to 400°F. Wash the potatoes well and dry thoroughly. Pierce each with the tines of a fork to keep the skins from bursting. Bake 1 hour, then cool on a rack until comfortable to handle.

2. Cut a thin slice lengthwise from the top of each potato. Remove the pulp, being careful not to tear the shells. Dice the potato pulp and set aside.

3. Combine the potato pulp, chopped onion, and chicken stock in a saucepan and bring to a boil. Reduce heat and simmer, covered, for 10 minutes.

4. Spoon the mixture into a blender container or food processor, add all remaining ingredients except the chopped chives and potato shells, and blend until smooth. Cover and refrigerate until cold.

5. Pour ⅓ cup soup into each potato "bowl" and garnish with chopped chives.

MAKES 6 SERVINGS
Each serving contains approximately :
Calories: 65   Cholesterol: 4 mg
Fat: 2 g   Sodium: 120 mg
* assumes skin "bowl" is not eaten

Vichyssoise in a Spud Bowl.

POTATO SALAD IN POTATO RINGS

The presentation of this potato salad adds an interesting dimension to a buffet table. The old-fashioned picnic-style potato salad is also the perfect accompaniment for a barbecue menu or tailgate party.

6 (12-ounce) baking potatoes
⅓ cup chopped onion
⅓ cup diced celery
⅓ cup diced red bell pepper
3 hard-boiled egg whites, chopped
¾ cup light mayonnaise
1 tablespoon mustard
1 tablespoon cider vinegar
¾ teaspoon salt
¼ teaspoon freshly ground black pepper
2 tablespoons capers

1. Preheat the oven to 400°F. Wash the potatoes well and dry thoroughly. Pierce each with the tines of a fork to keep the skins from bursting. Bake 1 hour, then cool on a rack until comfortable to handle.

2. Cut both ends off of the potatoes and then cut the potatoes in half crosswise to form circles. Scoop out the potato pulp, leaving the skins intact. Dice the pulp and set the rings aside.

3. Combine the diced potato, onion, celery, pepper, and egg whites and toss well. Combine all remaining ingredients, mix well, and add to potato mixture. Toss lightly, being careful not to mash up potato, until thoroughly mixed.

4. Stuff the potato salad into the prepared potato rings, heaping it up on the top.

MAKES 12 SERVINGS
Each serving contains approximately:
Calories: 145   Cholesterol: 10 mg
Fat: 10 g   Sodium: 544 mg

IRISH LAMB STEW STUFFED SPUDS

Nothing could be more perfect for a St. Patrick's Day buffet than this Irish lamb stew. In or out of the potato shell, it is an economical, easy-to-make, one-dish meal for any time of the year.

> 6 (12-ounce) baking potatoes
> 1½ cups defatted beef stock
> 2 bay leaves
> ¾ cup little boiling onions
> ½ cup diced carrot
> ¼ cup finely diced celery
> ¾ teaspoon salt
> ½ teaspoon freshly ground black pepper
> 1 cup shredded green cabbage
> ½ cup frozen peas, thawed
> ½ cup diced cooked lamb

1. Preheat the oven to 400°F. Wash the potatoes well and dry thoroughly. Pierce each with the tines of a fork to keep the skins from bursting. Bake 1 hour, then cool on a rack until comfortable to handle.

2. Cut a thin slice lengthwise from the top of each potato. Remove the pulp, being careful not to tear the shells. Dice the potato pulp and set aside.

3. Heat the stock in a saucepan over medium-high heat. Add the bay leaves, onions, carrot, celery, salt, and pepper, and cook until the carrot is tender, about 10 minutes. Discard the bay leaves and add the cabbage, peas, reserved potato pulp, and diced lamb. Heat thoroughly and pile into the prepared potato shells.

MAKES 6 SERVINGS

Each serving contains approximately:

Calories: 140   *Cholesterol: 33 mg*
Fat: 3 g   *Sodium: 372 mg*

TWICE-BAKED POTATO AND RAISIN PUDDING

I wanted a potato dessert to round out my totally potato table when it occured to me that rice pudding with raisins was one of my favorite desserts—so why not a potato and raisin dessert? This unique dessert certainly is a conversation piece. It is also a marvelous side dish with baked ham for an Easter menu.

> 6 (12 ounce) baking potatoes
> ¼ cup nonfat (skim) milk
> ⅓ cup sugar
> ¼ teaspoon salt
> 1 tablespoon ground cinnamon
> 4 teaspoons vanilla extract
> ½ cup raisins

1. Preheat the oven to 350°F. Wash the potatoes well and dry thoroughly. Pierce each with the tines of a fork to keep the skins from bursting. Bake 1 hour, then cool on a rack until comfortable to handle. Keep oven on.

2. Cut a thin slice lengthwise from the top of each potato. Remove the pulp, being careful not to tear the shells. Dice the potato pulp and set aside.

3. Put the potato pulp in a food processor with a metal blade. Add all the other ingredients except the raisins and blend until smooth. Transfer the mixture to a bowl, add the raisins, and mix well. Transfer into a number 7 pastry tube with a tip large enough for raisins to be piped through and pipe the "pudding" back into the potato shells. Bake for 20 minutes.

MAKES 6 SERVINGS

Each serving contains approximately:

Calories: 130   *Cholesterol: Negligible*
Fat: Negligible   *Sodium: 108 mg*

Irish Lamb Stew Stuffed Spuds.

Twice-Baked Potato and Raisin Pudding.

SPARKLING FRUIT PUNCH

¾ cup frozen unsweetened orange juice
   concentrate, undiluted

¾ cup frozen unsweetened pineapple
   juice concentrate, undiluted

½ cup frozen unsweetened apple juice
   concentrate, undiluted

6 cups sparkling water

Combine all ingredients and mix well.

MAKES 8 CUPS

Each cup contains approximately:

Calories: 121   *Cholesterol: 0 mg*

Fat: Negligible   *Sodium: 8 mg*

PARTY PIZZAS

SAUCE

1 medium onion, finely chopped (1½ cups)

2 garlic cloves, pressed or minced (2 teaspoons)

¼ cup finely chopped fresh parsley

2 tablespoons water

2 (6-ounce) cans tomato paste (1½ cups)

1 teaspoon dried oregano, crushed with a mortar and pestle

½ teaspoon dried basil, crushed with a mortar and pestle

½ teaspoon salt

¼ teaspoon freshly ground black pepper

4 eight-inch Herbed Pizza Crusts (recipe follows)

TOPPINGS

1 medium onion, thinly sliced (2 cups)

¼ pound fresh mushrooms, thinly sliced (1 cup)

1 cup thinly sliced green bell pepper

1 cup thinly sliced red bell pepper

1 small green zucchini, thinly sliced

1 small yellow zucchini, thinly sliced

1 pound part-skim mozzarella cheese, thinly sliced

1. Preheat the oven to 425°F. Combine onion, garlic, parsley, and water for sauce in a saucepan and cook, covered, over low heat, until soft, about 20 minutes. Remove from the heat and add all other sauce ingredients. Mix well. Allow to cool to room temperature. (Makes about 2 cups.)

2. Preheat the oven to 425°F. Spread ½ cup of sauce evenly over each pizza crust. Arrange vegetables decoratively over the top of the sauce. Bake for 10 minutes on the lowest shelf of oven.

3. Remove pizzas from oven and cover the top of each with the sliced cheese. Return to oven for 10 to 15 more minutes, or until cheese is melted and starting to brown. Remove from oven and allow to cool for 10 minutes before slicing.

MAKES 4 EIGHT-INCH PIZZAS

Each pizza contains approximately:

Calories: 920   Cholesterol: 66 mg

Fat: 29 g   Sodium: 2,217 mg

Painted Fruit Plates

1½ pounds frozen red raspberries, thawed, drained, pureed, and strained to remove the seeds

1½ pounds mangoes, papayas, or peaches, peeled, pits or seeds removed, pureed, and strained to remove any lumps

1½ cups low-fat ricotta cheese

¼ cup plain nonfat yogurt

3 tablespoons sugar

1½ teaspoons vanilla extract

Assorted decorative fruit pieces (use your imagination and the fruits in season. For example, apple wedges dipped in lemon juice to keep from discoloring, apricot quarters, blueberries, cantaloupe balls, green or red grapes, kiwi slices, orange sections, peach wedges, pineapple triangles, plum wedges, raspberries, strawberry slices, or watermelon balls)

6 (8-ounce) plastic squeeze bottles

1. Pour ¾ cup raspberry puree into each of 2 squeeze bottles. Repeat with mango puree.

2. Combine the ricotta cheese, yogurt, sugar, and vanilla in a food processor with a metal blade and blend until *satin* smooth. Spoon ¾ cup into each of 2 squeeze bottles.

3. Use your imagination. Paint your plate with the red, yellow, and white "paints" in the squeeze bottles. Select shapes and colors to please yourself and place them on the painted plate to create your very own design.

NUTRITIONAL VALUES WILL VARY DEPENDING ON FRUITS AND QUANTITIES USED

1 tablespoon of fruit puree contains approximately:

Calories: 6   Cholesterol: 0 mg

Fat: Negligible   Sodium: Negligible

1 tablespoon of pastry "cream" contains approximately:

Calories: 25   Cholesterol: 5 mg

Fat: 1 g   Sodium: 20 mg

Recipe Index

Index

◆